GALAXIES IN THE RAINDROPS

Galaxies in the Raindrops

Poems
by
DONNY BARILLA

BOOKS

Adelaide Books
New York/Lisbon
2018

GALAXIES IN THE RAINDROPS
Poems
By Donny Barilla

Copyright © by Donny Barilla
Cover design © 2018 Adelaide Books

Published by Adelaide Books, New York / Lisbon
adelaidebooks.org

Editor-in-Chief
Stevan V. Nikolic

All rights reserved. No part of this book may be reproduced in any manner whatsoever without written permission from the author except in the case of brief quotations embodied in critical articles and reviews.

For any information, please address Adelaide Books
at info@adelaidebooks.org
or write to:
Adelaide Books
244 Fifth Ave. Suite D27
New York, NY, 10001

ISBN-13: 978-1-949180-55-8
ISBN-10: 1-949180-55-7

Printed in the United States of America

Laura,

You will forever be in my heart

Gathering pine cones in my palm
I let them crumble,
Fine dust upon the wind.

Bath

I tread through the silk, gushing waters;
swift the breath upon the breeze sweetens across me,
gently I lather and soak.

There roams a pulse within me as the waves
dampen and the warm air blooms.

You drift beyond me.

I soothe as the salts covet your hair, full body.

I delve into your nakedness as the rippling tensions
of your flesh mimic the stroking wind.

East

Across the tan tread of the scorched field,
I walk this earth as layers of crust upon crust.

The maize crimped and fell, broomed to the ground.
In a haze, I follow each speck of tossed, flickering dust.

I glance my face, reddened and baked, asking for water;
I recall the juice of the empty creek,
I recall the rivulets which tendered the edge of the brook
as sweet soft soils suckling my heavy boot.

In a dash, I turn and face the coolest
mumbling breeze of the east.
With the glazing sun, I sulk through
the cool morning breath.

Rye

The pasture softened, bled in muds
along the sprout and shoot.
The breeze angled across the cool, burn of my tender face.

I spoke to the shadow of the reaching oak.
In reply, I listened to the muffling wind.

As the shedding leaves drifted in dew upon the ground,
I watched as her blouse filled in the wind and took
to the beds of each leafy pile, tans upon browns.

By the quiet chase of afternoon, the softest of understandings
glimpsed upon us and the deep of the wheat fields
lathered against the bareness of our legs
and the joust of the flickering branches doused upon us.

By nightfall, you dissipated into the vapors
stretching upon the turning spread of the heavy river.

Amidst the sliver of the moon,
I tread through each pocket of rye.

Seeds

The seeds burrowed in the pitch of darkness.
Among the endless tread into the deep,
I relish among the soils and all their mulch and mineral.

We awoke to the soundless crash of the sun
which strode along the stream and flooded
the banks well into the brim of softness.

Together, we stood and knelt into the slicing rapids
and balanced across each pebble and stone.

When the evening came and the moon
flickered through the dripping clouds,

I opened myself to your thin lips and walked
eagerly from flooding edge to open cove,

Slick, the dancing brim of silver light
slapped cross the salted liquid
so tender and alive.

Night

Into the delicate, breath slips as satin grooms
across the well scented room, bathing in pale light,
I fumble my thoughts into each stretch
for the pampered moonlight
jousting through the bay window and all its quivering,
clinging mist.

I roam the breadth of her.
I walk the shoreline as foams tread
through every inch, every grain.

Now, the sky hovers in scarlet,
I wilt to the hush of soft skylight.

The chill moans across the room and I lend my thoughts
to the shuddering wash of the tender sunrise.

Moonlight

She slithered across with every touch of dampness.
I reached across with the warmest breath.

Along the rim of her flush, pink lips,
I relish to her supple cove;
alive, each wilting breath demands me.

As I snap the trembling sweats of her skin,
every plum gathers for me at the base of her tree.

I collect a few and continue on through surface
and the crescent moonlight.

Hyacinth

The hyacinth gathered in purple clusters across the grassy hill.
From there, I wandered deeply into the woods
and filled the leafy, tanned leaves with
the tug of my eager boot.

Across the distant meadow, coming nearer,
I began with the tender sun.

I tell you, I speak of the majestic sky
which fattened in the sauce of a blooming apricot,
I felt so close to the openness of your pale breasts.

Then, calmly, I dredged my hands through the madness
of the late Autumn pollens.

I sulked into the lively snip of each falling flower
and deepened my way to the puckering wind.

Softly crouched at home, I begged upon your lips
and slept in the rivers of lulling slumber.

Dream

I fumbled across the dusty earth and found
the ribs tucked with each bolder and rock.

The spread, roaming hills cluttered in pines,
opened into the trench and valley-
smoothed into the sweet thighs which
quiver and waver upon the wind.

I felt the lick of the midnight sky
as silk robes swabbed across me.

Into the murky green pond,
I stepped gingerly and knelt to the press of soot and kelp.

On the edge, sprout of the onion grass
flickered with each damp coating of trembling dew.

By morning, I fled to the thicket where barley roams.
I found the delicate trail and trekked to the pasture
where the sun danced and softened beneath my feet.

Seagulls

Wrapping around hip, thigh, and burrowing groin,
the yellow, pale yellow dress rose so
subtle with the tender wind.

The breath of her laughed as each drop of tangled water
trellised along both neck and freckled chest.

Soft colors of melon, grapefruit stained gently upon her
thin, calmly spread lips.

I burrowed through each fiber and stitch.

Well into the giggling swoon of morning,
I paved a delicate path to her flickering,
trembling abdomen.

In the breach of day as nightfall swabs
through in all it's impurities,

Donny Barilla

the salts of a distant wind brought the seawater
in an approaching gale.

Standing in the meadow, facing the crescent moon,
I heard her moan n the passage of each seagull
courting upon the warm gown of a tepid night.

Peach

Quiet peach hues, the sliver of the moon
sank beyond the passing treads of the late Spring sky.

I soak among the grip of the wavering fog.
I soothe in the dripping patterns of a sweet mist.

Each flicker of moonlight prowls along the moistened
earth and shouts through the bones buried in fertile soil.

I creep my way to the havens of mud
which fasten to the endless pulse of my brethren.

By the thickest hour of nightfall,
the moon hides in the haze of a mumbling howl

Which brooms across the treetops and scatters
the crisp leaves.

Clouds

Into the mulch, I rose upon a fragrant, flowery flush,
so damp, the petals reached for the thick press
of each cloud designed upon passing drift.

Through the tight finish of the grasses dewy triumph,
I stepped in careful measure.

Followed by the warm winds, floating
in a rise of the bread, heavy yeast,

I finished this trek on the roaming probe of early sunshine.
Swift, I reach you and watch you drift away,
lost in the crumbling clouds.

Waist

The tremble of your soft pale legs, awakens
beneath me and roams as torrents to a sulking stream.

I lull to the gushing waters, soothing
to my waist, as the licking
current moans past and seasons unthread
with every moving pollen
gripping across my face.

My touch approaches you in sauced and burning riddles.
I fondle each answer and retort.

Now, alive and dripping in threads of running water,
we fasten to the soft earth which proves worthy
to each press of heel and toe.

With the groan of the rattle and flicker,
each twig and heavy branch,

Donny Barilla

I feel the passing winds tug through my
ears and sauce along my patterned hair.

The rise of the once dripping fog and
bloom of the scouring mist,
I now see clear to the meadow from
where we walked upon our way.

Autumn

I tread upon the earth, basted soft in the color saffron.
Close, the crows screamed aloud and rose to the cultured sky.
I spoke of each wing and feather
which motioned me to a new fracture of the passing breeze,
breath which bloomed beneath my heavy face and torso.

These rivers roamed through the green carpeted forest;
here I drank the icy chill as the muffled winds
tangled my hair in rivets and knots.

I am torn to the flirtatious ferns as they danced across my feet
and tickle as the hem of a skirt and blouse
grazing across the ribboned valley of my chest.

Silent and grasping in energy,
I walk the leaf covered soil while each fading bud dug
into the heavy floor.

Rain

Rain slapped the well prepared earth as the slithering
mud perched in slides and coated the endless bones.

Rising from the asphalt, the steam hushed and rose
as the incense of a chapel and thunder rang as a fastened bell.

Bloomed into the fresh scented mulch of morning,
I spoke to the orchid and lilac.

Soft winds swabbed across the wrinkled
caverns of my aging face.

I smiled as the mint leaves webbed
through the pooling ripples
which danced upon the nearest pond.

I stood for a moment, then continued.

Red

The moon slipped behind the threads of passing cottons
which hide as a full naked breast.

I fastened this goblet of milk and perched each sip
upon the crest of my quivering lips.

Fastened to the shadows of the croaking breath of morning,
I listened to the impromptus of the rising mouth of the sun.

From the lasso of the circling wind,
particles of motioning aroma
swelled to cheek and jaw.

Into the fullness of breath, wools and satin stitch, I trembled
through the tender passions upon the
breeze which scoured past.

Crisp, the dampest air softened my arms and chest.
I walked until the mourning dove called to me.

Donny Barilla

There pronounced a rhythm, the sky
wilted as the summer apple
and tender rain dripped in heavy flecks of red.

I drew the fulfillment of Summer deeply
into the depth of my lungs.

Peak

Clouds. Smoke trembles across the mountainous curves,
pronouncing as the jagged rocks speak to each wrestling pine.

I lean, kneel near the chipped coarseness of the cone
which settled in the needled bed of the earth.

The centuries brag of their wooded rings and sobbing wetness
as the ancient rain reoccurs.

There sliced a tiny brook which slithered
down the mountainside.
I quickly found it fresh, chilled to drink.

By the earliest morning hour,
peak to valley sauntered with fog.

I deepened to the thicket of the spreading woods.
I carried the gasping breath of day as it settled
into the corners of my lungs.

Joust

Dry, the river stitched, sewn shut, I followed
through the chiseled trembling of the
dusty wrapping arms of Summer.

You called to me and I forgot to turn and face
the voice of each particle of passing breath.

I followed the mountain path
and threaded my way along the warm winds,
growing, brooming colder by step and
tamp of these heavy boots.

Joust of the highest peak,
I trembled and thought of you.

Masquerade

Softened by the pulsing wind,
the flickering of my fine, limp threaded hair
groomed with each tug and pull.

I found the wrap of your arms, tight
as they pressed and dampened each tender
touch of her breasts which absorbed me.

The sky slanted and lathered us in rains.
I witnessed the drench of the skyline, boasting purples
which sulked in ribboned, fallen, cotton clouds
brooming across us as we thickened
our way through the fields.

Our moment touched as a masquerade,
wrapped in the coiling winds
of madness which swooned into the fleshy indigo's
of the pressured sky.

Spruce

Browned fibers of the tender spruce
leaned to the throbbing sun.
Soils fattened to the fallen needles as the forests breath slowly
tugged them across the woodland floor.

I savored every scent and tucked closely
to the saps of the noble pine.
Together, we danced upon the cones which chipped, rattled.

In a wild drift, the aroma of the endless woods
swept across my bust, my arms and tightening legs.

I turned in a dash and watched
the tumbling, tossing logs stretch the river which gushed
and muffled into the shaking waves.

Along the deep of the coveting forest,
I leaned against the heavy tree which
tore, threw to the suckling sky.

Bones

Chiseled, the maw of the mountain
chewed through the descent
of lofting clouds which sank from edge and ridge.

I followed the most narrow path.
I dug my boots into the cliffs and
scattered woods of the pines.

I spoke of liveliness as the mists soothed across my skin,
spread along my face.

Thick smoke lingered in want as the
summit made proclamations,
the highest peak threshed through the
breath of the thinning air.

Gripping the arm of the sycamore,
each splinter of wood burrowed fabric and hem.

Donny Barilla

Pressed, leaning against the coarse trunk, I sat
waiting for the leaves to gather about me,
collect my weary, aching bones.

Phantom

I sank my fingers, thumbs into the
cushion of your loosening blouse.
Here you spoke of breath and the patting mist
which gathered in streams along the windowpane.

From each gripping corner of your mouth, edge to edge,
sweet salve dripped and pooled about your chest,
freckled from clavicle to breast.

I held the shell of your hand, palm
tight along the map of my hand and softened to every pulse.

By nightfall, I absorbed to the boldness of your nakedness.
I danced my arms, abdomen and ribs into
the majesty of your apricot flesh.

Into the muscles of morning light,
I fell away and walked the endless halls of an endless field
and pasture which sank as the deepest trail,
leading me home.

Oak

The glare of the swollen moon
rose above the horizons brim,
settled along the fattened colors of navy and heavy pink.

I smiled upon her,
placed my hand along the edge of her slender shoulder.
Flickering dust glimmered through the fullness
of her auburn hair.

I unraveled the words which stitched
their way into the meadows
of my mouth.

I felt the chiseled statues of her fabrics and design.
Softly, she loosened in foams and mist
which gathered beneath and sulked as the wetness
of the oak, rained upon in the thick, roaming hours of dark.

Blouse

I stumbled upon the rock and soil of the earth.
Moisture clung as a web, damp and humid.

Gently, I tugged through the silks of your skirt,
I walked endless into the meadows, filled with rows
of barley, dance of the sun.

The blouse snapped buttons and fell as pebbles,
gathered on the fertile ground, moaning.

I lathered in the soaps of your breath.
quietly the birds landed, breathlessly.

Now, the grip of the trembling winds
wrapped about the old lines of my face.

From the creek where you stand, ankle deep,
I drink and drift the edge. Nearby, I watch the waving arms
of the elm, sulk beneath the breathing, loafing clouds.

Hill

I followed the threads of the fields bloomed with heavy grass.
I smelled the graze of the onion sprouts,
spreading upon the lofting wind.

Set on the pull of the roaming hill, I paused
and wavered to the mass of the oak,
the dance of the fallen acorn.

I waited until the glaze of nightfall and
smiled at the crescent moon.

Each color grew tender in the shades of dark purple
and the press of heavy blending navies.

From the deck of my home,
I sulked in remembrance of the suckling night.
damp the dewdrops of morning swam through the fields
and bulb of this stretching hill.

Spot

Into the muds of the April thaw, I
wrapped the fingers of my thick
hands and gripped the chewed bark of the birch wood.

I felt the paste of the trembling branches as the madness
of the sky descended in coming rains.

She spoke to me through the clouds as soft wind
tumbled my hair from loose to free.

Every particle of surmounting dust
gripped the sky with terror.

I closed to the descending fog and
dancing mist which sauntered
to the press of my tender face.

Alive, the rain pinched each spot of earth as
I sat quiet beneath the moaning tree.

North

I dripped in the fragrance, soaking about me
as I tread through these towering woods.

I looked; the pines stabbed their way
to the deepening skyline.
Slowly, the fog licked my shoulders and bust
as each dewdrop smoothed over in patient verbs.

With falling mist, I shattered each
mold which suckled upon me
in whispering maples which stretched through the silent
hush of tempered wood chips scattered across the ground.

Heading north, I trampled along the perching spruce.
Sweetly, I breathed the pine tampered mountainside
which hugged breath and spice as I lost, walked endless
into the hidden trails.

Upon the mountain peak, I glanced and witnessed the next
mountain peak, then another.

my tingling flesh sought the richest soil.

Waltz

The crisp, chilled wind flickered across
the back, base of my neck.
I walked the open field, dripping in pollens
which burst and flooded the air, threaded from the pods
as they roamed across the spindling
breath, fallen from the tender sky.

I loosened myself as the pebbles tamped.
Silent, the arrows of the midday sky soaked in rhythms.

In the hours of night, I danced to the pressing gauze
which trembled through each grass sprout and tangled weeds.

By the film of the hour of four o'clock to five o'clock,
I soaked in the presence of surmounting daylight.

I shifted my face to the dripping pink horizon.

Eagerly, I waltzed to the trail leading home and fastened
my feet in slow pursuance.

Acorns

Acorns, I gathered in the palm of my grip.

Sweetly, the wind thanked me and flickered
through the chestnut hues of my hair.

I lifted my sore heels and moaning arches.

Walking the elm ridden forest, I scattered
each nut and bowed my head to the earth.

Brook

I soothe from the coarse wind from above, swooning
the directions, north to south, west to east.

Lost in these mumbling winds,
I sulk through the rendering leaves

as they tumble and groom the mulched soil,
lofting across my weathered shoes.

The patterns of the swelling sun
throb across the pale blue sky,
threaded with the whitest clouds as they spread in cottons.

I motion my directions to the passing brook.
Here, I stop. Sensitivities of the white rippling caps
move me to the highest gushing ground.

Hunger

Rain pummeled and smacked the earth,
once coated in clays and spread with crusted soil.

I lay upon the smooth heavy stone.

I gathered the water which molded to the wince of my face,
now, pulsing in the quietest drip of the fattening sky.

Soft glaze of the pale sulking moon, every dance
of the ribboned heavens tears patterned
along my pasted body.

I heard the hunger of the once dying earth
as leaves, weeds, and fumbling grass

deepened into this press of wild night.

Robes

The highest peak, slumbering in the softest moss,
spread and thickened beneath the nakedness of my feet.

I walked through the shattered winds, tumbling
against my mumbling flesh

which begged for wheats of the valley's haze,
enamored in dripping fog from the clouds

which surround and depress against the groin,
blooming against the thighs of the pasture and field.

I begged for the humid, dampness of her mouth.

Into these meadows, I walked and ground the grains
beneath me. I absorbed the pulse of the panting sun.

In the nights mischief, I loosened the
robes which surround you.

Pond

The pond sat filled with silence.
Looking straight, heavily upon the water,
I drew scent into the caverns of my lungs,
breathing the lily pads and murky kelp.

She unraveled before me, the dancing wind,
the floods of a wrestling pile, slouch of leaves.

Points of the maple leaf soothed to the breathing water.

Leaving, I walked several miles.
I opened to the patterned rain which pampered,
opened to the descending sky and clouds.

Realms

There sulked passages to the starved realms;
rattling branches where leaves shook and scattered,
fallen in the carpet of woodland covering.

I listened, yet could not hear.
Rain dripped from the gray gnarled sky,

earth sipped in the throat of the thirty
mulch and dry pebble, rock.

I entered swift and watched the heavy moon swell.
Feeling this dancing breath, the bud, pod, pollens and leaves
took to the sky in a mad spirited tempest,
rolling through the shrub and bush.

I sliced my way to the fumbling creek.
I felt the crisp path of the swift wind as I stood.
Moments of clarity and softness dampened me.

Walking the edge, the red maple towered each
as the bark, riddled as a map, offered rest and shelter.

Blue

I watched the crackling blues moan through the black
canvas of the night's sky.

She opened herself in rain and fell upon me
as would the weight of her torso and naked breasts

pressing with a ginger touch, yet relevant to the madness,
each heavy raindrop, stinging the open glare
of my flesh.

With thunder in her voice, I grew damp.
Eagerly, I blended with the sauces of each cottony press
and dredge of each corner.

I felt the tapping of her fingers which drenched
as the tremble of my hands shaking beneath the heavens

covered me in the freshest scents.
In retort, I whispered to the dance of her wilting, soft ear.

Wild

I lay upon the earth, covered with sprouts and wild flowers.
Near the meadows edge, I softly dreamed of tender flesh
and rain soaked hair.

Touching her slippery shoulder,
madness courted and thrashed
across me, laughing in riddles.

Sunshine behind the wilted patch of grass
curled in as the wheat beside the blooming wind,

I slept here softly, resting my swimming head.

By morning, we forgot. By morning,
we danced in the fullness
of the meadow.

I groomed her in kisses and we sat silent by the clear, chilled
muffling voice of the swaggering creek.

Descent

I sat quiet by the stream.

The earth I walked upon, trembled across,
offered the fragrance of sweet mint.

The scent filled deep into my lungs.

Slowly, the scampering breath swept through the thick fog

as I smiled and treaded further into these soil laid meadows.

Tossed, the stick fell quickly into the roaming waters.

Paused for a moment, the sky, filled in splashing navies,

crunched clouds passing behind the bulb of the moon.

With the descending sky, I revealed my
soothing chest to the trembling wind.

Tribute

The stretch of this pregnant soil, swelled in tribute
to the lusty tamp of my mud packed earth.

Sweetly, I fell upon the willow and wavered with each branch.

I puckered to the throbbing moon as I touch each
delicate bud, tender and soft.

As I leaned upon the dancing, falling
winds, torn from the heavens,
I reached for each raindrop which slanted in ribbons.

I thought of this moment so slowly, I departed quite alive
with water and mud slouching about me.

Yellow

Slick, the juice as pulled from the plum, the nectarine, filled
the goblet of my jaw and seeped across the brim
of my mouth.

I awoke, softened to this touch.

From the garment, gingerly revealing
the paleness of each breast,
I soothed to a silent press.

As the laughter of her giggling mouth,
lungs deepened across me,
the patterned wools swept in heavy fragrance.

As the lemon dripped in tender butters of pale yellow,
I drank from the majesty of each mouth.

I yearned for the stint of morning.

I strived for the calm of the rising sun
and opened the passages
of tender sleep.

Violet

I entered into the breadth of these warm filled skies.

Sweetly, the dance of the passing pollen
drew film upon my
tender, eager flesh.

The dancing violets trembled against
the wind and suddenly,
tore free as the dampness of the grass
clung to each sodden
leaf and fallen twig.

I lusted to the freedom of the sun which pulsed
across me in rhythms.

Fevers of the break of day, slung fragrant pods
as they broke and roamed along each touch of my
spirited skin.

Donny Barilla

Into the pressing slant of the moon,
the Summer moon,
I felt the breeze stroke me as I smiled
to each quiver of the meandering flower.

Aromas

I gathered the breeze in my fist.

Aromas flung, filtered across the flickering winds.

I gathered my belongings and walked my way home.

Pollens flew swift to the sky.

*Full and open, this orchid
posed sweetly before me.
I felt tender between thumb and finger.
Petals fell loose upon my chest.*

Pollen and Pods

Alive in the dredge of the pollen and dancing pods,
she drew her skirt to her thighs and wandered
through as the seeds slapped, stuck to her powdery flesh.

As I followed so close, I answered her in ripples,
touching minuettes sliding with each forefinger.

She stopped for a fracture of a moment, her palms
dug deep to the cushions of each trembling thigh.

A few hours past, the sky drugged it's way.
The apricot and watermelon sky dripped upon us.

Together, we opened in the blasting sprouts
and weakened as the dusts swelled about our bust,
our quivering groins sapped relentless.

Cavern of Life

I look to the pink gems of her milk filled breasts.
Quietly, her face tensed. Sweetly, her jaw opened so gingerly,
breath slithered as the fullness of gauze taken flight,
swelled beneath the warm winds.

By evenings end, I looked at the mirror fogged
traces of breath -hieroglyphs.

Smiling, my fingers danced about the
width of her fleshy waist.
Into the door ajar which leads to madness,

I bloom full to the ripeness.

In a retreat of infancy, I sizzled upon this cavern of life.

Strobe Light

Her soaked, roaming flesh
washed into the endless eddies of the endless
ocean. The strobing light glanced pirouettes
which warmed upon nakedness of her freckled flesh.

Moans of her, labor lapsed a thousand years.
At last nightfall, the hooks of her toes
burned sand, the color of gold,
each gushing wave pulled me ashore.

We opened. We swallowed the water from inlet
to the throbbing cove.

I watched as she drained the colors from my face.

Night Visions

I flexed my vision, sight along the bends and contours
of each muscle on her shoulders and back,
as a field of sauntering wheat.

Her scent grew from aromas to a depth of spices.
Her hair swayed as a tapestry, welcoming
for a journey; hair full as the meadow
      alive in the fullest bloom.

She warmed the deepest pockets of chestnuts;
crackle of the nutty flesh, I removed myself from her,
quietly I fell aslumber and pulled fast
into the depth of my crisp linen sheets.

Forever, I hear the slippery grasp of her breath.

Silent Verbs

I touched her lips, scarlet paints
slithered through the evening
hours, so quiet, damp. Moisture gathered across my chest
as verbs slung their way with a soundless hum.

Earlier that day, I threshed through the garden.
Weeds piled in a soon to be deceased mound.
Rich fertile soil wrapped along my fingers edge
as the musky scents of Spring flung to me.

In the height of yesterday's rain,
I crimped my mouth as she walked by, opened
to the crocus and alive she knelt to the passing creek.

With clouds fumbling to the earth, I gathered my tools.
With the deepest of breaths, I placed her
garments upon an endless bed and burrowed into
her sweats and pulsing lips.

In the Field Alone

Slowly, I drew pulps from the ripest of plums
the drizzle of the nectarine.

Moment after moment,
I grew full as the juice veered from the corner of my lips.

There stirred a fractured yet endless second.

As I lay in the green grass fields, clipped and groomed,
I felt the sky swab me in the most eggshell white.

The cloth wrapped around the burn and sting of my groin,
so tenderly, I felt the ointments soothe.

The lone depress upon the patch where I lay,
slowly wilts back to shape in a gash of wind.

Watching for the Fox

I watch the red tail fox slip through the bush and trees.
I angle my face to the soft pulse of the moon,
The rings of the moon.

Patient.
By morning, the dash returns to the blitz of daylight.

Thick in reds, the stoplight penetrates
As I hear the beast beneath shrub and flower bed.

An image of you flurries into my mind.
I start the longest walk home.

By nightfall, I lay with you and rejoice
In the meld of your nakedness.

As She Danced Alone in the Woods

She danced in rhythms.
Into the deep of the wood, she soothed
upon the clover and moss, nude her feet moved silent.

The tender moon coiled across her breasts
as the fullness of the leaves collected at her feet, calves,
and the triumph of her thighs.

Fingers twined with fingers,
her hair flew into the tumbling wind.

By the thick of nights end, she rested, slept
along the side of the scattered pine needles
and breathed upon the scent of the saps

Flourishing from the nearby maples.

In the depth of madness, the oak
shred a basket full of acorns.
alone the branches cried.

Solitude

Upon the mountainside, I dressed in the thinnest linens
stretching across the valley and slope.

Roaming in these cottons which fall from the bounty
of the tender skyline, I thirst.

I beg the icy spring for a snip of cool water.

Later that night, I lay o this blanket and pillow.
I turn to these visions of her and feed upon her
tender breasts.

Full night, I am surrounded in fog.

Alabaster Flesh

She moved with each rippling breath upon her alabaster flesh.
Cool chill of the hands, digging thumbs, the curving fields
pulled at the threshold and offered the sweetest grains
blooming into lusty soils which dampened.

Within the ranch home, the scent of breads
loafed through the air.

Adjacent and flushed in the next room,
I sat by the snap and sizzle of the burning pine
burrowed in the fireplace.

Now, early Spring, and I watch the ghost of her
tug it's way through the ancient home.

By the joust of May, I can see her soothe through the fields.
I can witness the nudity she wears, robe
falling upon robe of the earth.

Madness of a Spring Day

Leaves brooming, lathering across each inch of the
Woodland, the tokens roaming through the forest gown.

I watched as smoke, moisture soothed
across the passing stream.
Gentle and enticing as the blouse of her
Whispering and falling to very wave, ripple,
I absorbed the draft and swallowed in
the waterbeds drowsiness.

Donny Barilla

Now, into the deep of Spring, I knelt by the towering oak.
She fluttered about me as the wind shifted and grew colder
By nightfall. I opened my mouth to the dash and drizzle
Of each lancing breath where dew surrenders to the earth.

Alive in this web, I crossed the nearby plains.
Grass clipping clung to my boot and cuff.

The source of all growth taunted and tempted.
In from the distance, I listened to the blackbird sing.

Echoing Breeze

I walked through the meadow, thick
with white flickering dewdrops.
With the snap of a leaf, I placed the droplet upon
the tip, edge of my tongue and explored the universe.

Further, the shed of the bark, falling by the lone pinetree,
I dug my fingers, palms through the
scraps of the previous year.
In a gust, I smelled the aroma of the earth.

The wind took to the leaves and pulse
from twig to reaching branch.

I felt the moss and cover shroud about me
as the nakedness of my body took to the echoing breeze.

With a sharpness, the pine needles tapped into my flesh.

In a moment, my flavors fell as a fleece to each angle
of the forest chips and mulch.

As I Joust the Forest

I rest as the enigma asleep in this forest,
I roam from edge to edge.

When my breath dissolves upon the wind,
I send you mist and scatter lints of fog
gently upon the dirt, clay floor.

Stream passing, I offer you the groin
treading wet across the basin drudged mud.

Searching the nestle of nuts and cones
even now, I ponder the swelling pride of your breasts
as they fed the breadth of the earth.

I follow each step of each foot
as you burrow above me.

Licking the elm leaves and maple and oak,
I slick my residue in the pinpoint of
the morning's trembling dew.

Blossoms

Shed, the blossoms of the weeping cherry tree
gathered upon the slithering stream.

Swift, I scooped one in my hand and placed
the slice of the groin upon my tongue.

Quickly, I slept until nightfall only to awaken
and thirst in the pouring gash of madness.

I gathered my shoes and socks,
I gathered my shirt and jacket.

Into the breath of the pouncing deep of Spring, I
walked until the evening groomed upon me.

Flavors of the flickering dash of meadow
passed me in heavy temptation.

Timber

I nibbled upon the pulp filled plums.
Juice gathered in the cup of my mouth,
Filling as a basin of the most perfect fountain.

My eyes peered to the west as the dying sun
grimaced across the slender horizon.

The sweat of the threshing winds, swift rain,
sopped across my face and torso.

Looking for shelter, we parted and the moans
of each surmounting breeze lusted inescapably.

Drained, there was one sultry draft which slapped in rhythms
and now, fresh into the dry winds of night,
I sulked to the plump of the moon.

The timber of this sparse gathering of ancient trees,
I rested here, into the inviting earth.

By the Lake, Time Spent

The slap of the wind, crest across the bountiful lake,
I whisper upon the breath of the waters edge, I loosen
into the press of every gushing wave; hair pulls in fullness
as I grow to the sauces of this heavy pocket.

You slowly wade in your fallen blouse, skirt swimming about
the thresh of your ankles and feet. The buoys of the endless
shorelines sulk to us in creams of madness.

Upon the glamor of the fat of the moon,
we walk the pebbles and onion sprouts which gather
along the edge, slithering foams pull forward then retreat.

I kneel to you as the kelp loosens upon my soft freckled skin.
You answer me with moans surfing the
moisture of each passing breath.

Gales from the West

The beads swelling upon the nakedness of her breasts
threw a gust of flowery spices,
alive from twitch to pulsing gland.

In the absence of togetherness, in the dampness of apartness,
so tenderly I swam about this room
where I witnessed her last,
the swelling thrashes pounced about these walls
where I strived for her in the serenity of gestures.

Yesterday, I walked perpetually in the fatness of the glen.
The drift and dance of her lilacs flooded.

Small depresses rested about the earth of the garden.
Here she lives in the heaviest of drifting scents.

GALAXIES IN THE RAINDROPS

Upon the wind, I felt the pulse of her as the ground
I sifted with fingers and palms gently
traced pirouettes about you.

Heavily in the gales from the west,
each breath you made sauntered forth
in echoes of partnership.

Place of Rest

Post to post, the thick fingers purged into the soil
so alive in this place where flesh rests and the scent
of each petal of each flower scampered across the wind
and filled my lungs to a fullness, lathered in aromas.

Walking home, I watched the mourning dove
flutter, flicker with her partner.

Seeds grew sparse as the wind washed through
the dance of my hair, fine and limp.

Sitting by roadside, I loosened the crimp of my feet.
In a flash, the broken glide of morning sun moaned across
each sliver of crouching tree and bush.

Full

I covered her nakedness with the cleanest of linens.
The spice of her soft hair filled the room
as I tendered to the fruits of her breasts, goblets filled.

The dampness of her creamed froth and milk,
the pillows where she lay, loosened to the clever
nook of fist and thumb.

By the hour, early in midday, she unravelled.

I tugged through the thick voices of her moans and purring.
Upon the dance of the aroma, she wallowed beside me.

Scents Aloft

The lilacs roamed with the corousing breeze.

Edges of the wilting taste upon my tongue grew damp
With the pods so alive.

Tucking my hair beneath the wools of my cap, I traced
my fingers to the petals realm where sweetness aroused
and flavors gathered about both nose and lips.

I stroked the bulbs of her as the breeze tempered to a lull.

Next year at this time, I could smell and taste her
as she wandered through the woods of walnut and oak.

Chapel Bells

Lounging with the humid press of her taut lips,
the ache of the wind glanced across the thirsty fields of maize.

Levelling myself to the heavy moisture of her ripe breasts,
the cloud fell into this partnership of morning.

So sweetly, I lost my way from finger to grooming
stride of the flesh she bore.

Cultured and blind, the thick wave of her tender abdomen,
I wallowed to the gestures of blind and the starved.

Now, deep in the thickets of afternoon, I can hear the bells
crack from the chapel so near.

I stand and walk to the edge of town and strike a match
only to plume the smoke to the recently
refined breath of wind.

Looking for Home

This valley, spread alive in the lime jades
where the sprouts and grasses plume upon the fattened breeze
both temperate and soft,

I dipped through each patch and weed
only to be born with this sweet precision.

I swallowed the clouds as they fell.
I soaked into the cottons which sulked
the edge of the meadow
roaming upon meadow.

At valleys end, I stood with an appraisal.
I held a close value to the mountainous stance.

Each slope and jagged boulder enticed
me to my treasured home.

Evergreen Woods

Temples. The spruce of the evergreen woods tickled
to the belly of the descending sky.

Pine saps drew a calm fragrance to the sweetness of the air.

Snapping crunches of wood chipped cones
depressed beneath my boot.

The trail mumbled with needles, crouching and tunneling,
as the fur trees softened the breach against the wind.

I swore to the dance of this heavy forest, "I dig
my fingers into your soil as these fragrances I will not
abandon."

The swagger of each branch soothed with nectars
moaning through the woods.

Moonglow

Behind the vanity she open her pulled hair,
absorbing the delicate moon, she giggles to the ices

of this frozen night.

There oozes tensions as I relish in her nakedness.
Together, we dethaw as the snowflakes
groom upon the ground

salted from the ocean spread, I can smell her spices

which loft about the cabin where we crouch and tamp.

In the mold of these moments,
I warm with these delicacies, moonglow upon her
full, milk filled breasts.

Overflowing Bowls

The sky, filled with mist, spilled as an overflowing bowl.
Drizzling white dew collected at my burning lips
as the mountain reaching in the south
        crawled with each spreading cloud, cold as cottons.

I reached within the pockets of my jacket,
withdrew a soft plum and fed these gnashing teeth.

Looking pensively, I soothed and admired the caves
which stretched across the cliffs face and opened
as a gathering for silk webs and floundering fog
        creeping along in the most distant howls of
each slant and monument face, chisel and mad rains.

I faced the direction from which I came;
I swallowed the pastures creek water and listened
to the crunch of grass beneath my feet.

From Waist to Feet

Along the strolling hills and it's deepening path
I watch as the moss soaks and coats the pebbled edge.

I breathe the snap of the cool chilled winds.
nearing the gathered scatter of ponds.

I drown in envy of the way you use to soak
and swim from feet to waist.

Now, the rains brew in evidence of the thrashing sky.

I huddle beneath the broadest of trees and drink
endlessly until my mouth loosens and madness subsides.

Fragrances

The rain dried and left the crops baron and tired;
each of the dew beads on tassle and bud
drew a fine misty flavor along the remainder of the wind.

Walking the edge of the soaked field
I chewed the mint leaves and stood back
to the neighboring woods;

I became so alive in the ashewood trees
I smelled a smoldering campfire as the swish
of the crisp, tumbling leaves paved my way.

Evening now, I reached the old farmhouse
which was chipped with white paints.

I stood back and admired the stretching ivy-
the blossoms of the tiger lillies pounded
their scents through the clever air.

Almost Summer

Into the glen, the aroma reached and spread
through the thistle and mesh of the wild flowers.

I softened myself and rested upon the stump
both crack and ancient.

By noon, the scents and scurry of the wind
wilted as the press of my legs tamped

Along regions of the richest soil which held
glimpses of nearing Summer and surmounting heat.

Soothingly, I traced my fingers through the grass
and I smiled as the warmer air surrounded my face
      and the tangle of my beard
bloomed to the ash colored clouds overhead.

With Scents around the Room

I ran the tips of my fingers through the spiced bloom
of her dark brown hair, filled with tangled aromas.

Softly, I untied the folds of her cotton shirt and coiled
my eyes to the cove and ocean of her back and shoulders.

Her alabaster colored breasts cupped as a chalice;
I could hear the mourning doves
scurry through the bird bath

while the snapping wind whipped the window
      by where we lay.

By the Ocean

Evening, the sky tosses it's cloak
threaded the patient colors: pink, apricot,
navy and the dying white.

I stood so still and watched my shadow fade
and thicken along the sandy, pebbled beach.

The fog horn was the moan of a woman
disrobing before bed.

I followed the arch of the slender moon, the silver threads
glinted upon me as I watch the buoys

wrestle with the salted water and
I felt the foams tug upon my foot and calf.

Spring Waters

The hills in the southern reach
sit stripped and bare.

Quietly, the leaves collect as a carpet;
motions along the rocky earth -trembling.

After finding the trail leading to the gushing spring,
I gather crisp waters in my mouth and drink heavily.

Alone here,
I feel the dancing wind.

These leaves crimp beneath the sole
of my weathered shoe;

The sun glances in the west and I
leave as light begins to fade.

Cluttering along the ground, each leaf
grooms as I smile and taste the fullness
      sloshing in my belly.

Loss of the Willow Tree

Surfing winds, white snow penetrates the forest floor.
I hear the branches brag of their bareness and deepened roots.

The frosted blankets swell as the flakes
gather and slope into mounds;

The smash of this bright Winter sun
      pounds through the tugging wind.

I rest upon the chipped and worn porch, watching
the gnarled reach of the birch wood mourn

into the rushing, cleaving winds.

The freeze of this season, mourns the loss of the willow tree.
Last Autumn, the soft branches threshed so proud.

Resting with the Blackbirds

The corn fields roam through the softest breeze.
Quietly, they stretch to the sun.

I trace my hands along the rows of stalks,
the husks loosen and tangle.

I perch upon a heavy, thick rock;
the earth beneath me whimpers to my slumber.

I soak through the breath of all seasons as gentle
threads of my hair tickle my face,
the fibers along my temple gather sweat
       a salty droplet of dew gathers.

Blackbirds dance through the air.
Each beak and wing rapes the tender maize.

I stare into the setting sun,
fumbling to the western sky.

Lakeside

The lake beneath the eastern hill
threw waters which purred and moved
as a slithering trickle of rain, gathering
by the splashing sun.

I cast my sight as the boats swam.

Softly, I traced my fingers and thumb
through the wiry ash of my beard.

With a dancing breath of wind, I heard,
I listened to the crows on ledge and shore
moaning to the slight chill, combing the air.

By the midday slouching sun,
I counted the murder, ever changing
like the ripples and gush.

Slicing through the Trees Roots

My fingers bloomed across her chest,
freckled as the leaves of scampering Autumn,
puzzles along the grass meadow;
I can still hear the branches moan
        upon the tempering winds.

So gently, I lay my temples upon the breads
of her fragrant breasts.

Into the deepened roots,
there pulses a moisture
which breeds both soil and clay.

I whisk my teary eyes to the sulking, evening sun.
My fingers dampen to the endless gush of each
endless river slicing through the yearning trees.

Hands through the Forest Ferns

Her breath sang across me and deepened throughout
as the pulse of my veins throbbed;
my eyes weakened to a glance as the tensions
of my temples tightened as leather.

I walked upon the forest and smiled
to each tremble of each fallen leaf.

When evening shrouded the sky, I peered,
I looked to the waltz of the wild flowers
which motioned to me in the senses of a passing
fragrance; I heard the fluttering ferns.

I touched each leaf of green and so madly,
I thought of her and the creamed color she shadowed
through the cottons of her shirt, quiet and alive.

Rest by the Slumbering Log

I lift my palms to the opened winds
and gather the scents of the distant mountains
which pierce the sky as the thin clouds lift.

Walking the endless trail,
I listen to the speech of the heavy earth
as I soften upon the breeze.

Now, resting, I hear the voice of the robin
as I lean the base of my head
upon the slumbering log.

Her song sings of abundance and roams
through each patch of grass and gathered
bundle of leaves.

Dust

Dedicated to: Larry Merkle
I melded to the earth which crooned beneath
and sang in countless voices of breath and trembling wind.

The trees reaching where my towers
which grew to the smash of the pale morning sun.

I smiled upon the moss which lay as a carpet,
a pronouncement of rest and regal glow.

When I listen, as I always listen, I can hear the ghosts
of the earth beg for shadow and dust.

Gathering the sands of the most remote and distant
ocean, I drink the clever reach of the brine
which soothes upon my lips.

I will return to you in the softest muds
which breed me as a satchel.

Climbing the fog trimmed wind and the mist
dripping from the farthest mountain,
      I speak to you of togetherness.

Walking in the Meadow at Night

The path roamed across each fattened field.
Crumbling earth lay peppered along the edge
where the deepest green weeds tugged to the sky.

Wind at my back, I swiveled and faced
the molding breath which pursed across
each grass blade and dead crinkling leaf.

Sunk in the depth of the meadow,
I grew upon the summit of the pumping hills
which stretched upon a distant skyline.

By passage of night,
I thickened my way to the sinking cloud, thinning gauze.

Slumber in the Depth of Night

There whispers a depth,
a crooning touch where I reach through you,
I bloom upon the harvesting winds
fumbling scarce into the heavy glimpse of night.

I see, I touch the wheats of your fields and pastures,
you wear the palest powders of Winter's threading blanch.

I witness the fullness of your milky breads.
Quietly, I rest upon the slope of your slouching breasts.

At the crevice of morning,
the silk gesture of your purring voice beckons me
to the sauces of each nimble touch.

Early Morning

From the satin threads of your bloomed, black
tapestries, I pressed my eager face upon each
edge of your sulking hair.

The mist fell upon the earth as the fallen clouds
rose in perfect measure.

Beyond the forest,
I walked the pastures which boasted
the silent trails;

I spoke to the fading fog and smiled
upon the glisten of dew as the rock
laden path broomed across the closure of nightfall.

I pressed my face to the rising sun.
Late, the chills of cresent morning
drafted upon my shoulders.

Elegy

I sift my fingers through the webs of the finest mist.
I face the tremble of quiet morning.

In a soft moment, I turn and walk heavy upon the earth.

Shoulders Awaken

Resting boulders roamed the base of the southern
mountain, peering to the silk blue sky.

I asked the nearby maple tree, "How do you sleep so quiet
as the sun saunters through each branch and supple leaf?"

Leaning upon the arms and limbs,
I listened to the grazing wind
which broomed along the tender field,

Meanwhile I felt a fullness in the crest of my shoulders.

I watched as the leaves glanced upon
each, perched heavy rock.

Searching

The quiet breeze faded to a soft hush
as the glen threw so few wavering blades
of thicket, thistle and grass, I
felt the brooming wave of my hair hang to temple and cheek.

Upon asking the broad roam
of the mountains their spiny creeks and icy springs,
each question of glory and winded lust,

I turned my way to the ponds of the valley
which lay so softened,
I heard the murmur of each shoot and lily pad
as they trembled in their silence.

By the crest of the morning sun,
dripping in buttery heat,
the trail which fastened through the forest,

roamed as a splintered twig
falling near bush and motionless shrub.

Lastly, I lathered in the poison heat,
crimped for a snip of water,
and roamed for the furthest blast of mountains
which probed the most northern blanch of flake.

Ocean's Spread

I slithered my hand, my finger and palm,
across the brim of this goblet
which ran as river and the endless push of the ocean.

Her mouth opened with the trembling vacancy
of the most humid breath;

I sulked to the caves as I rested within
each scattering pebble and rock
soothing the soft press of my tongue.

In the quake of morning's dance,
I lay lathered by the foaming sea.

I sink to the cottony fog as the waves of her
raise me in press and sermon of the nakedness
of her soaking breast.

Valley

In chords, I reach my fingers through the soil
which surrenders to the peaks of mountaintops,
runs as a spread through the kneeling valley.

I remove a flower from the soft earth.
Gently, it brooms across my face.

As the day lathers me in pollens,
I dream of your pale, white skin.

From Ocean to Mountain Path

I turn to the east and pursue the stretch
of the heaviest mountain
bundled and cropped in rock and boulder thrown askew.

Midway, I rest by the poplars and soak through the threads
of the thinnest air.

I recall the soils in which I came from
as the fibers of each descending cloud sifts upon me.

The scream of the ocean, gnarled and swivelled, beckons
me in salts and song.

Tenderly, I lay my bust and hear the
sweet verbs as they thresh
through the vast gush of breeze and current.

Approaching Nightfall

In the vast roaming fields, carpeted in wheats
which hold the treasures of your waving hair, I reach
my fingers through the edge along your mouth
        and lips, tugged in wine and crimson.

The scent of your pulsing skin drifts across me.

I grow to you in fevers, waltz to each
glisten of white, trembling dew
as they paste across your chest, patient creams.

Into the tans and golds where you rise,
humbled, I sulk beneath -I listen to the scalding sun
and return to you in a blossomed breath
        across the open pods of each moaning hill,
where I will find you come nightfall.

I feel the laughter of her apricot skin,
together,
we stumble with a silk touch.

Chapel of the Woods

Clouds falling smoked along the forests trim,
leaves dancing,
I speak to the clinging branches which waver to me
as the breath of a drafty chapel.

Thin incense fumbling through each shrub,
tight mosses wrapped to stones.

I turn my face to the rise of the sun.
I face in wait -always east.

Softly, I disappear to among the webs of prowling mist.

Surrender to the Rain

Rain trembled across the fog dripped ground;
I awoke to the draft of each droplet on each of these
spring mornings.

Breathing the coarse cool air, the holly bushes
boasted of their thick green leaves
alive with the smallest of berries,
bent in the winds, quiet and so alive.

I sent my eyes as they roamed through the pasture.
I mourned with the snap of the arm
of the heaviest of oak trees.

With a patterned pinch and pouch of gathered rain, I
removed my feet from the boots which lurk inside
And I wait until the endlessness of approaching nightfall.

The fumbling clouds spilled each drop
across my feet. Patiently, I surrender.

Facing the Clay's of the Earth

Standing upon the dust of the raped, barren earth
I felt the tang of my sweaty, slick forehead
which pasted to each flickering hair, withered
        and cool.

A full bloom of the static sun and I returned
to the dead fields where I heard the thinnest
flecks and sounds of your fading voice.

Later yet,
I turned and faced the clays beneath me;
I listened yet heard no sounds.

Halfway home, the winds wrapped across me
as the temptations of the sun disrobed me.
Ever so gently, I fell to the mumbling earth.

Beneath an Evergreen

The earth was coaxed to slithering mud, so I
looked to a cool, heavy sky
finding clear, crisp rain.

I threw my eyes to the clever shout of the tree limb
softly brooding with the wettest soil.

I stand beneath an all reaching evergreen
smiling an hour later
as the bloated showers creep to a halt-
sauces flood within me.

Green Buds

I find a flicker in the broad
chest and torso of this maple tree.

The wind slaps and changes direction
as I smell this sweet aroma of the genitals

which burn from base to each strobing limb and blossom.

Tenderly, I suspend myself and scurry, find my way
to the green thickness of the mountain I love.

Looking to the low fields between each peak,
I think of her in the ripest of buds.

Watching Seasons Pass

Branches tangle and weave through with clatter
and moans as the woods dampens perching buds,
soaked in white dewdrops.

The sauces of the spiny river quiets
into the edge of Autumn.

Along the steeple of the whispering mountains,
the forest spreads as a weed, a sulk of the nearby moss.

Flickering greens wallow in the drip of the quickening winds
which dance in waves and humility. So lost in this realm,
I shatter my lusts for the silence of approaching Winter.

I gather my possessions and venture
as the peak faces north, a deepness of the scalding freeze
which shatters in each trembling breath,
the thinnest smoke.

Cold Spring and Separation

I lay upon her as the rise of the pinkest breast,
breads of the smoothest pulses.

Into the wash of this sulking cloud
which drips across us, quiet the mist pats on the breath
of each humid lingering steam.

The earth mumbled in a slight crunch
as we walked on the grotto, this vast stretch
of grasses sending a submission of defeat.

I can hear the flicker of the spreading wind,
flutter of the garden flowers.

Leaving this sacred place, I mourned each lull
of each rise, then fall of the cove
which deepened within her.

The walk home spoke of cold passings
where the breeze wrapped around me.

The Death of a Wood

I dwell in this place this woodland home.
The crinkling leaves whisper of their soothing
lusts as the roaming breath of Summer
lick each twitch upon them, the mildest breeze.

I stop by the silence of the fallen, shattered maple
which sleeps so heavily in the gentle tread
of a once used now forgotten path,
threaded through the pangs of heat and drought.

I gathered myself and walked to the river,
receded as the press of the sun,
by the edge of the once roaring rapid
I wedged a pebble between my naked feet.

Into the silent arms of the Summer's rash,
burning across each wilt and crimp of the brownest leaf,

I fled the groans of a dry forest,
the passions of life looked upon me as they fled their soils.

Wading through the Oldest Water

There rose a steam, gentle mist floundering
across the oldest waters.

With naked feet, I slipped quietly into the rippling,
slithering stretch of this plain face

Which blankly looked upon the thick clouds
treading so slow across the sky.

I opened my mouth and breathed the aroma
deeply into the vaults of my chest.

Standing there for several moments, I then returned
to the water's edge and lost the drifting, cloudy smoke

Which patted in droplets upon the awakening
film of this silent antiquity.

Birch Wood

In late Autumn, the leaves now fell
and each tree speaks of their nakedness.

I mourn for the shame of the maple
which drips saps and moans with each press

of the slapping Fall wind.

I walk through this field of scattered trees
and muffled leaves.

The white birch wood stands dignified.
from stem to wavering branch,

Taunts of the approach of Wintery treasures
cloak across the dead earth.

I walk further into the closest woods and smile
as the barren snow begins falling.

Howl

I spoke to the woods which stood
tall and broad in triumph of the mid hour of Spring.

In temptation, I roam these trails and rest at the end of day.

I can hear the howl of the wind
as they tore through the canvas of each treetop.

By Cherry Tree

The elder woman looked upon the blooming cherry tree
and slung a smile through the timid air.

Each petal quivered as a few shook to the passing breeze.

The earth was soft and tenderly quiet.
She passed, I heard the 'rap tatting' of her cane
as the breath of eager Spring groomed across her.

On the dance of cooling nightfall,
I heard the chant of every floating verb.

By morning, the shattered glimpse of pink and reds
tugged across stone and sulking grass.

Quiet Moonlight by the River

The drape of her hair, chestnut hue, fell across the neck
and bloomed in fullness and scent.

Rivers poured across her as the flicker and lather
of her skin held the throbbing
press across each timid rippling gown of water.

In the gasping end of Spring, I went to the prowl
of the river majestic.

I cupped the threads of my fingers and drank
as spirits rose.

Upon the wind, I heard her trickling voice
whimper through me the thrash of her silken threads
moistened me in pulses
      of quiet moonlight.

Oceanic

Warm blue light scattered through the sky,
crackling residual water ripples bent in curves

as she molded and sank beneath me.

I open myself in the most silent flesh as the corners
of her mouth trembled so slow.

In the first hour of morning, I looked
upon the water as each wave
spread upon the naked shore.

The patience of her bending, powdered skin-
the sky combed and fattened in dark grays
as the blitzing lights of this maternal thick water
danced beneath the quivering hands and the touch of me.

We spoke through the hour of morning
as the rash of deep night shook into the beyond.

Incense Rose

Raised roots stitched their way into the soils
of a crumbled earth. Trees spoke to the passing
breath as ventured upon by the wind.

Their rose a smallness, a flowered dance which shook
each weed, shrub, and bush.

I watched myself dissipate as the dust of the driest
soil; blooming fog as fallen from the tall peaks
from the southern reach which threaded through
these tender valleys, I awoke and held no voice for you.

The blossoms crept beneath me as I spun in the vapors
of a mourning sky.

I rose as incense. I fell upon the clays of the earth.
Feeling the heaviness of your eyes, I return to the soothing
tread beneath your shoes.

Flash of Rain

I cross the trail, covered in rocks, which asks
so kindly for the touch of my shadow.

Midway across the thick, heavy rubble
I hear the smack of the rain.

There burns a groan from the winds thrashing
across the leaves and crackling twigs.

I ordain myself to the rhythms of each dew drop
landing upon the skin I suspend to
the waves of this heavy wash.

Now, clear again, my thick spread of shadow returns.
I can see the scour of an amber skyline
      -slicing across the horizons edge.

Stretching Glen

I slipped my way across the tense films
of her abdomen. Softly, I mourned the patter
of the rain which held us in gestures
much as the floods of the grass filled
gardens pulsing beneath this window-
Cracked and rattling. I thought of her
slithering upon these sheets, quiet and damp.

The space between these pillows
sulked as an endless cavern.

I swam through the dense moan of this
battered house. Each cloth of each linen closet
and trunk, wept as I held it's tears.

I can hear the almost silent footsteps of your feet
when I cast my sight upon the stretch of the glen.

Vanilla and the Bead of Wax

This silent room flecks in dust
as I watch her slip down the narrow hall.

With light, the almost melted candle
sheds a bead of wax. I pause to the scent
she left, spices and the tangled perfumes of her hair.

This blanket we wrap in as a cocoon,
speaks of sorrow and joy.

These pipes behind the worn thin walls
moan of companionship and touch.

With all the softness and powders of her nakedness,
I warm to her as she soaks in the glamoring flicker-
smoke and the scents of vanilla creams flooded the room.

After Dusk

Wide open, the field melds to the setting sun.
I watch her with ginger, soft eyes as she thickens
Each color and hue upon the slender horizon.

She disrobes and the black naked sky
soaks the earth as the most vulnerable cool air
trembles across and moistens.

I hear her voice as the crows begins to sleep
and the tangled weeds tempt the fingers of each gale.

Midsummer Rain

I walk the trails of the southern hills
which speak of the oldest and most lucid.

The dance of the Summer wind layers
upon each budding green
as they pucker and satiate soil and flocks of rain.

I awake in the hot breath of a fine and wet
silky air. I can walk in the tread of my boot

As each touch of dew throws a covenant with the earth.

The exhaustion of the fading height of mid season past,
I can find my way as the leaves upturn and crimp

Once again for the suckling rain.

Warm Breath

Clays of the earth warm beneath my naked feet.
by evening, the sun slices through the
evergreens, maples, and oaks.

As night floods the trim of this forest and spread
of the nearby pasture, I grab a fist of leaves.

With opened eyes and tension on my knuckle and palm,
I dredge my way from each slip of the dewdrop.

Skies buckle with the swiftest breeze.
Deep night crackles the trees and escorts the falling branches
as every wilted blade of grass begins to excite.

This place cups each water bead as the warmest breath
flickers upon me.

Bamboo

As the shadow fades
husk of the bamboo shoot,
I circle the row of bushes only to return
and smile upon the palest of jade.

This early hour of nightfall
shrouds as a cloak.

With each fattened shake of the apple tree
there roams spices of Autumn afternoons,
filling my lungs with trickles of sauces
and seeping nectars and pulps.

With early hours of morning,
I looked in return to the shoot
as the wood of the bamboo
suspends a dew drop, only
to release it to the covenant of this earth.

Emerald Mountain

The mountain held as fangs to the sky.
I shook myself from this valley
and trembled to the rock path rising in jagged
intervals.

Now, Winter swept behind me,
I draw close to the pine scented woods as they
bleed the color emerald along the base of this summit.

This green needle within my palm-
I find myself eager for the girth of Summer.

Sea to Open Cove

White shreds of rippling water glanced flickering light
from the moon as the shells and rocks sank to the seabed,
open and alive these foams whimpered.

I make way to the cove where small scattered islands
probe through the chill of nightfall and thin, the smoke
from every fallen cloud dampens my hair and face.

I enter the humid arms of fresh morning.
The pulse of the sea shatters me in early heat.

Soon, the clouds will lift as the fog will vanish.
Seagulls tread the wind and I hear each moan
from the waves as they smack the tender golden sands.

Thickening at the Heaviest Hour

I ask of you, "Graze the fingers of your hands
through the silk waters of the stream. Quietly
touch my face with your palm and turn your delicate
breath to the press of tender night as the crinkled leaves fall
and gather about our naked feet while the pebbles
find home beneath our heel and toe."

"Let the mist of thickening evening,
shrouding navies of the night's sky,
wrap and coil about us in silent ordination
as we return to streams and creeks
from which we came."

So tenderly, I open the vault of the earth
and smile to the pulse of the approaching moon
which lathers us in silver robes.

Donny Barilla

In the sweetest draft of morning, I can hear the dance
of the early pale yellow sun breach across the horizon
quivering dust across us in fibers and hems.

By river's edge, the moist nurture of the soil
soaks upon us in fragrances of the early trembling
dew as the clays turn to mud.

Looking for Home

Open fields, the sun tapped upon the meadow
which threaded the finest jade for sprout and grassy tuft.

I could smell. I could feel the approaching rain
slapping in the glen. I watched the mud suckle about my feet.
The waves of the overgrowth tempted
as the mourn of the sky.

I looked to the east and a well selected murder of crows
scattered across the low breeze which taunted both trees
and the fullness of my hair.

Into the width of the broad open pasture, where I lay,
trembling dances of light glimmered upon me.

I will wait until evening as the moisture
flecks across my cheeks
and drizzles from grasses, cupped in veins, to scattered nuts
falling from the heavy oak.

I found the thinnest of trails which sliced through the field.
So softly, each gust of wind soothed across my back.

*I listen to the sobbing sky, slowly
the winds shift from the north.
I gather the snowy frost.*

Rainstorm

Open palms, I gather a sauce driven from the lowest
of sulking clouds. I swallow these juices as the fevers
burn beneath my reddened flesh.

I turn my oldest face to the fractured bead
holding galaxies on the tip of each dewdrop.

Looking upon you, my fingers tremble
as I penetrate each groin and posture-
there swells a rouse in pulps and sweet salves.

I sweat to the pulsing rain.
I can hear the splashing waters, flapping in pushes
of naked feet.

Donny Barilla

There opens a flickering madness to the
set of the sun, I face the western
trimmed horizon and I watch the fields as they
cast their garments aside and dredge into the gash
of a heavy oaks which scatter and the muds which slip
down the hill, fumbled in porridges
tempted in a suckling breath.

Awakening in the Evergreen Forest

The trail, most thin, wrapped and bent
around the forested trees
as the pinecones tapped so close to my feet.

Listening to the soft winds, I spoke gently and awoke
to the canvased treetops. Each fluttering breeze washed
across me and soothingly, I unfurled to
the closeness of this morning.

Tumbling dust galloped around my boots.
I walked a far distance and collected dusts of this forest.

Each flickering shade of morning,
the long shadows and bending glamor of light,
peach and pinks which faded in a quiet softness,
dashed upon my face and I bent to
the path riddled in pebbles,
gathered in stones,

Donny Barilla

I walked this tender trail as nuts and cones fell so near
to the brow of my foot.

The wind touched upon my hair and I
measured my way from valley

to the green spreading cascading stretch of hills

covered in the mumbling grip of the evergreen.

I Left Her in the Morning

Grazing the edge of my lips along the softness
of your pale, full breasts, the winds patted so gently
at the looseness of the nearby window, I sank
along the valley where meadows began.

She smiled and I drifted to the open
grasp of the open breeze.

Her breath soothed as a warm gasp upon the corners
of the bed where I lay.

I spoke to her of the heat which rose where the thighs
of her tuft of wheats roamed across my lips.

I witnessed the trembling pouch of skin
which swelled in eager press and groomed in pastures.

The next morning I had left this place.
I wandered to the height of each ripe mountain
and sulking hill.

Light Fastened at the Break of Day

I sink to the trench of this fastened light
as peaked across the wave of the trembling hills
rolling hush of the maple and the elm.

Ajar, I open my quivering mouth and breath
the scent of the mint and the blossoming
yearn of the lavender.

Most soothing, the gusting winds pause in fellowship
at the cooled snip of my foot and ankle.

The great spread of the mulch and soil
awaken to the tread of my boot and gather at my tender face.

I seize for a fracture of a moment, then
continue on to the mumbling earth
which gathers me as a host
treading upon the bloom and scent of the earth.

At Valley's End

This valley, spread alive in the lime jades
where the sprouts and grasses plume upon the fattened breeze
both temperate and soft,

I dipped through each patch and weed
only to be born with this sweet precision.

I swallowed the clouds as they fell.
I soaked into the cottons which sulked
the edge of the meadow
roaming upon meadow.

At valleys end, I stood with an appraisal.
I held a close value to the mountainous stance.

Each slope and jagged boulder enticed
me to my treasured home.

The Songbirds

The fracture of morning bled in a host of purples
and shattered the calmest of pinks, then
awaited the butters and ambers
of the yellow and rise of the sun.

I swallowed the crisp breath of morning
as the pastures flickered with every stem and blade of grass.

I touched, felt, and absorbed the pulses
of this fever which surmounted each tension
burrowing in the depth of my throat.

Angling my narrow sight upon the sliver of the sky,
the bluebirds flecked and danced as I listened
to the croon of each morning sermon, tenderly awake,

GALAXIES IN THE RAINDROPS

The flutter of the sober wing, spoke to
the gush of each tender ear.

I slipped my palms and my hands
across the beard of my face.
I listened to the gasping wind which soaked in song
as I deepened in this trench of voice and vision.

Oak

The oak stretched from root to quivering bud,
tender, the finest color jade.

Resting, I looked to her and place my forefinger
softly upon her lower lip and watched as the leaves
danced to the breath of this field-
awake and soothingly alive.

Patterns of the leaves upon the grass filled floor,
I smiled to your most gentle mouth, I lay you in this bed
and sulk to the silence. A tremble stirs to the fullness
of each puzzled piece of leaf and nook of burrowed acorn
which fell and dashed through the leaves.

As I raise your mouth to my mouth, I feel
the tapping rain as it dampens the flesh
of crimping leaves beneath us and we suckle
each particle of wind.

Return to the Earth

I watch the steeple needle to the threads of the sky,
patient blues sulk in a drift as the clouds thin
and the late afternoon skies sink to the earth,
alive in the softest fog, every cotton stitch
spreads across the heavy soil.

I can hear myself breath as the humid graze
passes through my lips.

Fluid steps, I walk the glen and pass
the thicket and lumbering trees.

I mold to the vibrations of my lips and pulsing groin.
The breads of the earth soak across me.
I walk to the endless grotto and meld my way

to every fracture of the soft bounty I touch, yield
in the deepness of day.

Patience in the Pause of Morning

Together we rest in the rise of light.
Warm beams permeate; I gather my fingers
about the paleness of her tender breasts.

I groom with the softness of my pouches,
palms which rise to moisture and the temptation
of the most eager powders.

Further, I stretch across the travelling bend
of the whimper where her abdomen croons
to every touch and trickle of the water bead.

Slowly, I wait until the middle of morning.
The surmounting madness of pauses and threshing
coats, the fields of her soaking rains,

I dampen to each patch of the barley.
Soothing to each moistening brooke
      as the wind flashes across the fullness of her hair.

Spring Fade

I touch upon the gentle verbs of morning,
clouds flex to the grass and pebbles of the stretching field.

In depth of soft fragrances, the wild flowers
bloom to each corner of sprout and dance of the wind.

Tender and with softness, I place the edge of my hand
upon the fullness of your cream colored breasts.

The sky sinks upon us as the lather of the mist
weathers both flesh and strobe of our vision
      born in the breach of day.

Approaching dampness, I place kisses upon the pulse
of your tender mouth.

I deepen in the stretch of the heavy rivers and streams.
Together we fade into the quiet blush of Spring vespers.

Falling in Prisms

The tree branches shed dry, crimped leaves upon the ground.
Thrashing with my legs, my feet,
I stirred each flicker of dust to the rising wind.

So tenderly, these slivers and stems
gathered in the nearby fields.
Slowly, I walked among them and watched
as the warming sun fell in prisms and danced.

Past the Clothes Line

There swept fabrics roaming across the dusty wind,
heavy blankets and sheets clung to the clothes line,
I gather the sweeping scents; burrowing mint and fresh
clipped grass sulked to my awakening face.

In the evening, I walked among the hyacinth,
passed by the stout blooming thistle.

Into the depth of the wet grass, I tread the earth, soil
with each heel and sole of my boot.

Much later, still walking, I looked to the sky
and drew witness to the heavens and all it's navies.
I smiled upon the palest moon, then, headed home
as the pollens clung to my jeans, damp.

Dreaming of the Apple Grove

The breads of her whispered upon me.
Feeling the damp dewdrops of late evening,
she sank to the sweats of my temples and curve
of my straining torso.

There roamed a breath in the heaviest
of the late night hour, I deepened to her.

We rested softly by the apple tree.
Together, the pulps danced along the edge of our tongues.

Morning came and we vanished
to the glisten of the grasses which held no depresses.

The early winds swam through my thoughts.
I soon felt the press of the sun.

Forest Majestic

The yearn of the elm tree grew in a angled slope
tugging to the warmth and light to the sun.

In a tender hue, the lime and jade, each leaf fluttered
upon the most tender breeze

which soothed through the forest majestic
and filled each leaf, branch, and stem with breath.

My lungs doused their way to sulking scents
and stroked it's way across my pale, soft face.

Branches swayed as a tug to the garment bloomed
upon the fragrant wind. I stood soaked in this pulsing echoe

as it rattled through each opened pore
of each spot along each touch of Spring.

I Covet by the Fence

The fence, soak with the deepest tans, stood strong
against the pound of the wind.

Sitting by the roaming edges, deepening though
the richest soils, I sat in the heavy strobe of silence.

Gently, I felt the hair upon my temple flicker.
my fingers stretched through the nearby grass.

I watched, smelled the gusting scents
of the lilac bush as they pampered in a swivelling tug, toss.

Sitting so silent, the stitch of the wood burrowed
into the edge of my naked neck.

Into the brash wind, I calmly left this place and swept
along each garden glen.

Forest Fortune

After the rain, heavy rain, the soil
sulked, dripped in porridges.
Tender, the sun pierced the horizon in coral blue
and enticed with the softest pink.

Calmly, I stood by this dashed and quivering pond.
The sun crept upon this patch of water
as rays reflected in green kelp, swaying ribbons.

Kneeling to the edge, the moistest mud,
I traced the tip of my forefinger and watched,
this cluttered woods were told a silent fortune.

Together with this gnarled forest, I listened to the breach
of daylight. Several hours later, I wandered lost,
the depth of nightfall crept near. Prisms of the sun shattered

as I watched the skyline hush the verbs of the softest
croon, eager to my ears, creeping in tensions.

Pulse

I relish, consumed by the softness of her touch.
Roaming across the breads of her,
alive in the twitch and fever.

Next year, at the same pulse of day, I walk the valley
and peer upon the sulking forested hills.

That morning, I smelled her aroma
with the glance of the rising fog.

From the prisms, fracture of temperate day,
I soak into you, wilt to the breath you broom
across each quiet stalk and shoot.

Meadow and Mountain

I lathered in the soothing creams
which spoke of the foams slick and spreading
upon the sands of a distant shore.

The tiger lillies roped through the
current which drew sauces of a faint rain.

Wilt of the expended Summer grass,
each spear and blade returned to the dash
of emerald green.

Months later, I stood upon the mountaintop,
I gathered the eager raindrops, cupped
in the touch of my jaw.

I opened my tilting neck and soaked to each pulse

Donny Barilla

of each breeze and wave; the brash trellises,
thick the bulbous drops slapped in a lusty breath.

In the gasp of my mouth, I tasted the fertile earth
of the slant and fertility of the mountainside.

Into the calm dance of daylight,
I heard the crashing slap of wind
thresh in the loafing desires of valley,
pasture, and meadow jade.

Mist

By the heavy river, lotions and foams
gathered by the edge and bank.
I drew a thirst from the cavern of my chest.
Sauces stretched across the nakedness of my toes.
I opened myself to the patterns of the winds,
grooming upon the tempt
of every watery ointment, I stood to the weed
covered shoreline and turned looking upon
the soon drip of clouds and meandering mist.

Galaxies in the Raindrops

Ridges in my knuckles, swift these fingers roamed
across each trembling bead of her pale, powdered thighs.

Placing my mouth into her silent galaxies,
I heard the depth of her lungs

which soberly pushed my humid breath
into each pouch of her nape, nave,
and crescent shaped breast.

After I left the satins and linens of her bed,
I walked the narrow path, sizzling and pounding with rain.

I paused, listening so close.
In eager moans of each droplet,
falling from the plump of the clouds,

I heard the muffled groan of these galaxies in the raindrops.

Lost in the Woods

I walk the most narrow of paths.
Rain gathers about me in sheets, dripping linens
forgotten upon the clothesline.

Ferns scattered along the forest floor
wiggle to the wind and hush, bow to me
as I tenderly pass.

Although I am lost, the buttered sun
reigns in the east.

So sweetly, I love the breath of morning.

Wind surfs through my loose, fine hair.
I taste the salts against my lips and tongue.
By high tide, the world trembles at my mouth.

Fields of Rye

Near the red brick home, the magnolias perched,
issuing a dash of swollen petals and blooming fragrances
which tugged their way through the
tossing, resourceful breeze.

I burrowed into the black, metal chair.
Silently, the loafing jaunt of each open bud and bloom,
slithered across me as the dancing trim of moonlight.

For years at monthly intervals, she
sweetly dug her fingers, thumbs
through the mineral rich soil.

Now, the last Spring, I filled my lungs
and shook my chest and torso
upon the wind which threw to the softest air.

Donny Barilla

The depresses of her shoes and palms have faded.
Her lips upon my neck retreat.

I open myself to the pausing gloat of temptation
with nearby puckering buds which open as the tassle of wheat
flooded in the most distant field where you once walked.

As evening came, the chiseling blast of heavy gales
spun me into the shades of a dying prism.

Lost, for a stretched fragment of time, I gave myself
to the dance of the wind.

We met and walked slowly through the golden fields of rye.

Rule of the Northern Mountains

Into the evergreen wood,
mid winter trees colored basil
and broomed the ash snowy cones
as they dropped upon the needled floor.

I stood and quivered
as the northern chill
strapped across my face and burned
each finger of my naked hands.

I walked to the most remote
patch where sanctuary spoke
of the endurance of the cardinal
and the death of each flower and withered spice.

Donny Barilla

The sun flickered through the trees
and the shadow proclaimed itself
in vapors of light and a distant stretch
where the ice turns to sludge and the softest
muds suckle to heel and toe.

I turn my eyes to the most northern mountains and shake
as the sun descends while the white trimmed cliffs
speak of the heaviest faces of the deceased.

I watch with envy as the shadow splashes across the mountain
and all of nightfall sleeps in a blackened slumber.

Infancy

Into the depth of her arms, endless
fields of thistle and grass, she
opened herself to the creams of the rivers shore.
Foams pooled along as her full breasts
trimmed the fertile earth.

I lay my head upon the softest moss and she quivered
about me. I felt the snap of the torrents of the wind
whip across my burning red ears and cheeks.

Jaw and tongue supped upon the juices where I lay,
shuddering to the cold river and warming to the heat
of her abdomen, dancing as the rise of the yeasts
where the breads bloomed beneath soft cotton towels.

Donny Barilla

Soothingly, she fed me and in the portion of a moment,
I drank from her endless river.

By morning, the fields soaked from edge to edge.
Heavily, I wandered with my head in a
damp pasture which I covet-
soaked, my body relished in her sweat.

Magnolias

I placed the smallness of her hand in the palm of mine.
Warmth of the morning sun, I watched her sweat beads
trace their way from temple to neck.

I kissed them as they dispersed upon the edge of my tongue.

She quivered and exposed herself in shy blossoms
as the pink of the magnolia giggled with each petal
        and stem.

Fallen Gown

The heavens opened, agape as the jaw of the fallen clouds,
swelled in the puncture of the swollen groin.

I danced through the arms of the falling mist.
Soothingly, I wrap through the breath
of this cloudy descension.

I am opened to morning, the weather of the east
coils along this thinning breeze.

With the rapture of the creams of each taunt
of each pucker, I am seasoned to the voice where
the slickest touch draws sauce and fills
the satin robe with a lusty groan.

GALAXIES IN THE RAINDROPS

By mid morning, I lather these crimping palms.

I hear her voice as the slicing gasp of wind
brooms through my hair.
By the fragrance of noon and the mist fading,
I am so sweetly alive to the genuflect of dashing sun.

With every blanch from the sky, I
warm to the mouth of Spring.

As the Path Leads to the Greenest Hills

The path led as carpets of tan and brown.
Each snip of jagged rock wedged through the sole
of my weathered boot.

I heard the threshing oak trees which lined the trail.
Sulking as the dance of the field of wheat
which bloomed beneath the snapping breath
of a skyward lunge.

I placed a fist of acorns into the deep
of this pocket holding treasures
which chipped in the cask of each wooden nut.

GALAXIES IN THE RAINDROPS

Walking to the end of the dry earth where the slender road
met with the emerald hills,

I entered the wet splashing leaves and dampened
into the trusted mud. Shy, the rain pinched the fat
drowsy slumber of each tender mask of green.

Edge to Edge

I touched the vapors as they sulked from her mouth,
edge to edge.

By this mountain majestic, I watched these roaming breasts
offer nourishment from icy caps to threads of a green
fleshed landscape of crying trees.

Your milks return to the soil where you stand.
Swiftly, I speak to you as you gleem naked as the top
of the stretching mountainside.

When the clouds drape across you as a cotton garment,
I roam these landscapes, so alive and I search for you.

Woodland Green

Through thicket, shrub, and bush I tread into the deepened
and remote gathering of the forest.

The thick heat of summer thrashed each thorn
into the plump of my flesh.

I stopped and looked upon the trembling shards of sunlight
flickering through the swollen treetops.

As common, I stopped by the marsh, heavy bog.
I asked for you and received a glint upon the fattened kelp.

Although I was lost, I waded into the deep.
The glamor of the darkest shade of nightfall

Donny Barilla

rushed as a breeze which snapped the
twigs and rotten branches.
I searched for you and slouched in
defeat to the woodland sage,

which cleansed as I grappled forth,
alive the kelp whispered to me and offered a cleansing,
from thicket to dancing greens.

Neighbors

Upon the silks of the down bed, she shook
the garment loose in gatherings of slumps
which threw the freshest fragrance to the jousting
glances within the room.

With the walls rattling,
I spoke so brief, the breasts of her
pressed heavy upon my abdomen.

In the visitation which bled to morning,
I tossed my slacks and wrinkled shirt
quickly upon my body.

Donny Barilla

Outdoors, the greeting slap of the sun,
I walked the trail, deep into the meadow.
fading dewdrops wrestled to my boots
as the sprout and onion stalk gave way.

Approaching home, I slept in the dance of the silent ranch,
so open, the stiff air surrounded me.

May Funeral

As I listened to your breath, dirt swept the empty field.
I recall the voice you gave as I tread the endless path.

I knelt down and pocketed a stone in my denim pouch.
Moments past, the gales quickened and soothed
across my sunburnt face.

I smiled as the protruding rocks delved
to my leather torn sole.

Then, I turned my bust to the whimpering winds
and I heard you again, giggling upon the crest of my ears.

Night Affair

The fullness of her blouse, fell silent.
From thigh to the softest waist, I roamed across her
as wind pulls the wheat dancing in the wavering field.

Standing by the humble creek, I felt the moisture
of her trembling lips as each patch of grass
offered the sweetest dew.

I poured into you and kissed you in rhythms-
splash of the quavering moon.

I slid my hands across your belly and heard
the distant mountainside crash into the winds
of the widespread cove and blossomed sea.

With warning, the pinks and dredging purples
stretched across the horizon and spoke of daybreak.

Tenderly, we walked the glancing prowl of swivelling wheat.

Cocoon

There softened breads between us.
I soothed in the dampness of her touch
as the pollens scattered in this garden, so tenderly
I quaked to the spices of your neck.

The tiger lillies puckered upon each breath.
As night gathered, my feet sank to the press
of the earth which wrapped about us as a cocoon.

I return to you as the seed blushing across the eastern wind.

As Spoken from a Pasture

The dash of sun filled its way through the barley's dance.
The silk locks of her hair
bloomed in the softest hue and trellised across
the nakedness of my chest, legs and groin.

I filled my way to her thin, gasping mouth.
As I received her, I felt the earth rise
milking upon me in each color and pigment.

By the height of the middle of the day, I
soaked and lathered in your channel where the stream
meets stream and the grasses flood the edge.

You told me of a pasture where the moon
groans in every voice and the fevers of night's chill
swells the ivy and patch of mint.

GALAXIES IN THE RAINDROPS

I spooled about her and softened with minerals
which crimp beneath the tapping touch of her fingers.

Into the deep of nightfall, I watched
the haze of the fattening sky,
devour each blemish of the promising burrow
of winds grazing and pastures full.

Ancestors

By the announcement of the crisp sun, deep into afternoon,
the oak leaves whispered to me and pronounced
every phrase of every word, wild into the wind.

I tucked you beneath the wrap of my belt.
I savor you tenderly upon the tip of my moistening tongue.

Passing the graves of the grip of the earth,
I pass my Father's return as I pass his Father's return.

I hear the moans of the maternal womb
gingerly alive as the voice of her filled the breadth
of her daughters and the breadth of her daughters.

I walk this endless road
which combs the soil of our ancestors.

By days end, I return to the promise of the earth.
By morning, I shower as dust upon the earliest breeze.

The Naked Beach

Waves riddled in white caps, clapped against the stretch,
the soft curving shoreline which enticed as the waist
of her full naked body, alive in the laughter of dancing kelp.

Ankle deep, I softened against the slither of the beach
and soothed into the gritty sands of the beaches edge.

Winds tucked from the fullness of the sinking clouds.
I sank my sky whipped face through each draping
and each toss of salty breath.

Now the evening colors fade.
I feel her breasts, smooth into nightfall, groom across me
as the threads of her thighs
writhe in nectars and passages.

As the heavens drench upon me,
I sleep through every mist colored sheet of blossoming winds.
I fall in her fleshy arms and slumber.

Overflowing

Into the depth of the clothing,
garment and blouse, each tossed
the powdered scent where sunshine smacks
as the fields into a golden hum,
silk sound which throb through the tender breeze.

I dipped my way through your tense muscles,
sinewy strain, as the sweet taste of your hooking thighs
tremored across my bust and humid chest.

I surrendered to you as you fed me milks and creams.
I bent across you as the dancing sun threw it's robe
silently across the horizon.

You stung tenderly as the flavors of the emerald earth.
I stroked each satin finish of each inch of your soft skin.

I held each memory in the cup of my overflowing mouth.

Autumn Dreams in the Forest Deep

The rattle of the branches humbled
me with heavy crackling voices
which scattered the earth with leaves and acorns
both the color of tan and brown.

I leaned against the mighty oak, delicately
I fell to slumber and dreamed of you
as the scents of powdered fall
scattered through every
treeline and called for the smash of rain.

I looked upon you,
vulnerable in all your nakedness.
I touched your bloomed and full breasts
as they sank upon me,
opened and chilled as the passing breeze.

Donny Barilla

In the vagueness of this sauntering dream,
I searched the endless girth of the forest.

In a fracture of a moment, I suckled upon your fruits
and awoke to the thick breath of Fall
which soaked each vessel and vein of the tossing leaves.

Maple

I discovered the pebbled, rock strewn road which led me to
the full basin, fattened cove of the lake.

Nearby, the maple threw shadows and cooled
in the softness of it's ash gray cloak.

I sat by root and moss which soothed;
I drank each passing breath and quietly,
I ordained myself to the hushing
advance of this Autumn crown.

The sky grew pink and red at the end of day;
I felt the drizzle of a soft mist and became drunk
with the brew of each rippling wave which hosted

white caps settled with the tapping droplets
as I awakened to the splashing rain.

By the Creek

The horizon spread, thin lips which
perched the colors red and navy.
Turned, I opened myself to the most delicate breeze
which bloomed from the incense flouting from the earth,
a calm fog soon to surround my legs and waist.

Clouds passing, I thought of your tender breasts.
I soothed my way to the stream of
juice which gushed from you.

I accepted you in moisture.
I dranks the sweat from your smoothe brow.

The passage of evening riddled the sky.
Now, nightfall, I went to the creeks which coddled past.

I awoke to the paleness of your thighs.
I spoke soft of the brooming light as I drank from the streams
and curving rivers and we sat quiet by angle and bend.

Pact with the Crescent Moon

I look to the crescent moon.
Slippery winds groan past me.

I stand in the wet grass and speak of the fog which will arrive
deep into the glamour of morning.

Walking home, I wade to my thighs.
This early Spring dash of sun;

with the fellowship of the past night, I offer
myself in sharp blades and the stab of the stalk.

I hear the whistle of the branches which flourish
each leaf as they gleem their lime colored buds.

Again, I walk into the depth of night.

Reds and Pinks

Standing so close to the weeping cherry tree,
each blossom of bleeding pink drifts close,
surrounds me in delicate flavors.

Dancing moonlight, red moon,
I move myself to the white birchwood bench.

Suddenly, I stretch and tread to become part of this earth.
Dripping in the softest grotto, the
petals quiet me as a shroud.

Scenes from a Park

I withstand the bend of the wind;
into the gravel road beside the tumbling creek, I walk
into the arms of the low spreading clouds
which saunters across the water.

I sit quite still and feel the damp mist
wash across my face.
I turn a cheek to the trees which surround;
I watch as the pines shed their cones
in perfect pronunciation.

The red covered bridge rests so invitingly.
I look at the couples cross, crossing the plank
which suckles the trembling cloud-
falling into the brook below.

Secret of the Dancing Wind

Against the fullness of your naked lips,
I roamed the galaxy.

From buckle to garment,
I explored the deepness of the moon
which throbbed in rings and ushered forth
a tender canvas, navies and thick, heavy purples.

An hour later, I found the secret of the dancing wind.
Tender breath upon the quivering grasses.

The pollens flew warmly to the fields
where I once thought of you, ages ago.

Thorn

Nearby, the pond rested and exclaimed
the monuments and faculty
of the crying whispers as the wind blew soft.

Thick vapors from the low dark clouds
pampered their juices, fallen crystals
which soaked the earth in malts and minerals.

By days end, I whispered and mourned.
Every fallen petal lay in the groin of the earth.

Dripping to the Earth

The wind throated past beneath the purples and blending
navies which threaded from horizon to canvased treetop.

Resting upon the smoothest of rocks, I listened
to the frogs gallup past and the swallow of water
brooming upon the edge of the softest creek.

She met me here as the thin cottons of a fallen cloud
dampened and drizzled.

An hour passes and I swelled and became part of her.
I lay my swimming head along the curve
of her gentle breast. Quietly, we dreamt through
to the sauces of morning and found apartness and distance.

I stood, fully awake. The edge of my window opened
and allowed the trim and breeze as the spices of the garden
flooded past.

Each inch of the room stood bare.
I walked the glen and found flavors dripping to the earth.

Birchwood

I think of you and your satin bloomed skin.

Looking upon the birchwood tree
yearning for the sky, I loosen a tear
and call for each movement you throw
as a white slender branch.

Delved in the alabaster of this imagination,
I reach upon the wind to touch your breasts
filled in the juices of a plum, pear.

Sorrow blooms from this trellised bud.
Passive. I stand and walk a great distance
only to hear your delicate soprano voice tremble to the rattle
of the breeze.

Leaving Home

Tangled, I breath the western winds,
I breath the eastern winds.
I stand trembling in this bloom and dance of every fragrance.

I look to the mountain, deep in the north,
stiff with ice and pounding gales.

To the south I travel and search the forest
for brambles and quivering treetops.

So close to the nearest creek, I drink
as if the breeze blew warm
along the fields of maize.

I loosen my shirt and look behind to the
white caps and thrashing wind.

Into the Mist

Swift wind, the branches tangle and rattle.
Walking the grotto, pods open and drifting seeds
wrestle through my hair and face.

The last moment I saw you, you dripped in bareness.
Now, fully clothed, I watch as you walk
deep into the glen and garden.

I pardon the breeze.
Wiping my face clean, I turn and walk
further to the emerald grasses.

Standing above the strength of the buried rocks,
I walk into the forever dripping sheets of fog-
I disappear into the mist.

Traveling beneath the Winter Sky

I stumble into the praise of the eastern sun,
rising and disrobing before the wavering, hushing fields.

Wrapping my lips to the chilled, icy water
I smile so deservingly as you fall, trembling upon the earth.

Months pass, the arms of Winter, coiled in ice,
I gather my things and leave you,

buried in the moist, mineral rich soil.

The fragments of the heavy Winter skyline
bleed in pinks, soft pinks.

I turn to the east and walk endlessly.

Rest by the Lake

I relish in the fifth month, inches past Winter.
Soil suckles upon my shoes.
I kick the stubborn rocks, enticing
the clover and dance of the onion sprout.

I feel my pale face begin to burn.
Walking the furthest path from here, I
wade waist deep into the fields.

Days later, I rest by the slosh of the shore
born of the tender lake.

I will never find my way home from here.

Spring Laughter

I stand on the ices of Winter's past,
gleaming in layer upon layer
as the rings of the evergreen caked in frost.

Stiff, I hold the seeds in my palm and flush
each grain to the blanching wind.

Now, passage leaning to the end of daylight, I tamp
my breath to the choking breeze
I stand so alive in this fog dripping in departure.

Much later, past the frozen deep,
I loosen to the laughter of Spring breeze
and dance my path to the nakedness of sunshine.

Woodland Statues

The snapping branches cover the ground,
willows take upon the wind.

I lean my face to the cherry wood
-breath heavily.

Moments later, I walk into the thick of the woods,
calmly, I am surrounded,

Alive with tender scents, the might of the oak
crowns the forest floor.

An acorn drops and nestles in the pile of leaves.

Aware, the mosses lean against the chiseled wood.
Quietly, I deepen into these ancient statues.

Time in the Grotto

Petals of the magnolia
scatter the crusted, brown earth,
riddled in roots and pebbles.

Every shade of pink spools upon the passing breeze.
I watch them lift to the sky
and wash in colors, thread in the most patient dye.

Nearby, the pond suckles the greenest kelp.
I open my lungs to the passing pollens
which drift, then land on waters film.

Looking distant, the sky bleeds in pinks
and creamy lemon butters.

Wait

I wait for you in the nakedness of winter's deep.
Blankets unfurl and pass through,
across my burning feet of ice.

Now, Spring tempts me and I still
wait in the dew driven landscape.

I turn my face to the east and lust after
each graze of lifting pollen.

I worry to the haze of Summer and you have not shone.

Time Spent by a Passing River

Driftwood spools upon the bending river,
heavy the color green.

I reach into the passing water and pluck
the gnarled stick, grab with a fist.

The dense, thick air of Summer blends
across my sweaty brow.
Crisp, the blend of a damp breeze
patterns across the sweet air surrounding me.

I draw patterns in the dirt with the wood.

I tuck the tender scents of August and
sulk to the trim of Autumn
which waits in the sullen wind.

Night Approaches

Light of the crescent moon gathers on
my cream colored sleeves.
I gleam to the blossoming night
as tender wind breathes into me in the draft of evening.

I stand and watch as the crows gather in the maple tree.
Heavy winds, the murder drifts to the bow of the field.
Sweet breezes of distant pollens fill in my bust and face.

I look to see the black flecks stir upon the wind.

Pine Shower

The mountainside showers in pines.
Beds of needles rest next to cones, the chipped wood.

Powdery winterscapes dredge the white bloom, I think
of her and the pale nakedness of her breasts.

So close to the snow, I am warm against her freckled chest.

Her pink lips, full mouth tread across me in rhythms,
sounds of the mountains woods creek and groan.

By Spring, I wander the cascading hills and fall
in a fullness to the roaming fields.

I find you here as the gentle buds pucker upon the wind.

Watching the Willow in a Thunderstorm

The strength of the willow tree has grown old.
Now bending upon the wind,
I find it supple and unbreakable.

My fingers tremble upon the silks of her flesh.
I watch the skies thicken to the color of ash.

Here, the willow gushes with the pat of the rain.

I rest and watch as blue lights smack across the sky
from brim to brim.

Moments later, the gentle wood bursts into splinters.

I fill with sorrow.

I lean so close to the yellow threading candle.
Tenderly, her flesh dances about the room.
I pulse next to this sweeping fire.

Thickening Trees

Passing through this stretch of trees,
I smell the ripeness of the wood.

I touch the lather of the pine, dripping in saps.

Upon a tender breeze,
The leaves make way for the grooming sunlight.

By nightfall, I lose my way and rest.
Alone, this treeline thickens as I roam.

Mountain Pass

I follow the mountain pass as leaves
scurry across the floor posted with maples.

Into the blossom of my bust, nose and ears,
I gather these scents and sounds;
aloud, the woodpecker dances, the fumbling stream threshes.

I rest on the boulders by roadside and breath
the tight thinning air.

By nightfall, the mist weaves along my red, burning skin,
I gather the cool mist which threads as a web.

Tenderly, I sleep in these arms.

Perched

Into the spread of these gathered clothes
I hear the moan between these paneled walls.

I seize with my lips from roof to jaw
and open the gates to your sloping neck.

From the heights of these moist, smooth breasts, I
nurture and breath upon the spices of your skin.

Finding the loosened path to the vanity, standing broad
in the corner, valley of your room,

I grip each ridge and peak as I pass.

Later, I cloth in the denim and cottons
I brought to this meeting,
tenderly, I pass through the door
Entering the dripping clouds on this perched home,
surrounded in the voices of a warm Summer night.

Rest

Nearby the antiquated farm house,
the creek bled greens and kelps
Across the scattered tree beds;
the grass blew in flurries of the most gentle
breeze.

Into the deep of afternoon,
I peered to the sky, filled with strokes
of an ash laden spread of clouds,

I stood still with the slapping rains.
I felt the tender muds suckle my feet, ankles.

By evening, the creek rose to the rock and pebbled edge.

I stiffened to the rise of this grave filled field.
by morning, there was a glimmer of rest.

Absence

As I rest by the firelight, wax upon wick,
the fullness of this candle has faded and I
deepen into the wool capped covers.

Faint glimmering faded yellow light batters
across the walls and floor of this room.

I stretch upon this bed and sulk
as the fattened moon passes across the bay window.

Now morning, the threads of night
poise as I think of you and your absence.

Without you, I smell the fragrances of your trellised hair.

I gather the water, coffee, and mug as I
sit here looking into the distant stretching hills.

In the Fields of Spring

Spring warmth lifts the earthy scents from the mud
and groom of the tuft of grass.

By roads edge, the onion stalk flavors the wind.

Kneeling, I drink from the spring, dancing water.
Remembering,
I feel the chill of my feet as the breeze dashes across me.

Into the field, I bear the sting of my eyes
as the pollens flout from the bursting bud and pod.

I walk for the better half of the day.
I taste the sour snap of the fullness of the apple tree.
Gripping the plums, I think of her as she undressed
last Autumn.

Slipped Away

The quivering bead, shades of white,
slowly drips upon the gathering of red Autumn leaves.

From this monument of ancient oaks, I sweep
the forest floor with the press of my steady feet.

Swelling silvers of the blossoming moon
sheds the coolest light, flickering haze

of mist blooming upon the bush, shrub, and earth
pampered as down on a gentle bed.

I looked long, longingly across this bed of haze.
She reached for my arm as I recall she sat

gently beside me and kept her voice as the trembling
rings of the puckering navy, deeply statued in the sky.
I reached for her and slowly she slipped away.

Pausing to Ask a Question

Mountain fog rests trimmed as a crown,
spread thin as cottons, I look
peering to this mount in the east as the tip and crag
holstered the rise of the crumbling sun.

I walk to the west,
waiting for the setting sun dancing
in heavy blues, purples and oranges;
creams of this descent blooms the slumbering moon

as the meadows I tread through
narrow their way upon an elder log
resting from the fallen tree in the moist rot
of the field, soaked.

I look to you and ask, "Which way do I turn."

Dark Seeds

Moist night, dark as the seed of the fleshed, ripe apple,
I sink my teeth to the depth of night's cloak.

As the juice upon my chin, I look,
stand close to the trickling brook.

I wait. Steady my feet stand on the rocks edge.
I thirst as the white capped ripples of the passing creek
slowly floods this orchard.

Soft, the tender current fills each tree
with wash and minerals.

In a glance, the night flourishes to daylight.

Storms of Madness

The storm broomed the Autumn leaves,
now floating along the gushing river.

I heard the crack of the branches
as they meshed with the heavy winds.

I could not hear the whimper of my breath
as the dense fog fell, fallen clouds,

This cottony stretch of fading Autumn breath
lulled so still, I wept for the snap of each pine.

There sulks madness in these trees.
The trickling dewdrops continue to
dash upon the soaked earth.

I pull myself deeply into the forest
where all the usual noises now remain calm.

Candlelight

I slip, absorb into your full body;
the powders lift from each bend of your nakedness.
My tender mouth trembles with each slow, soft movement
as I gather these rose petals which drift about your feet.

I hear the gales from the north tamp;
upon the walls and rattling window
I pass my way through the bed
        and all the wool blankets
which wrap us in heavy warmth.

I turn to her and smile, she
flickers the candlelight which dances around the room.

The creamed colors of yellow and orange,
I swell to these gentle lights
as they smooth across her fumbling breast
and the dance of her quivering belly.

We toss beneath our drifting fragrances and spices
which lift from our flesh.

After the Storm and All It's Humid Breath

I stopped by the willow,
Thresh of each tossing branch, wild from the sky,
Breath of the Summer breeze as the heat
Submits to the approaching storm.

Close, there rests an oak, marveled in strength
And fending the panting breath of the gasping
Groan from the northern mountains.

I crouch beneath the eaves of row upon row,
the heavy lumber.

In the thick of deep night, the rain ceases
And the branches still.

GALAXIES IN THE RAINDROPS

I walk upon the sodden ground
As the gathered, fallen leaves hush
upon a brooming tremble of wind.

Passed through the bloom of the rattling storm,
I am swabbed by the humid touch of fallen rain.
I continue on through the depth of the clamoring woods.

Struggling for Home

I hear the voices spill, mumble through this pinewood forest.
I walk through the branches and slip along each pine and
sap which blanch against my soft, tender flesh.

As I deepen into the shadowed wood,
all soothes to silence.

Gingerly, I step upon a nutty, chipped cone
and this echoes through the halls of tree and branch.

Moments later, I find the lost, narrow path
-I walk my way to the meadow where I rest.

Eager, the winds roam at my back, I stand
silently before my thick wooden home.

Breast

Into this blemish of torrents,
I position my face to the gray ashwood sky.

Sweetwater drenches upon my face
as the lakes and ponds simmer to a tread and dance.

By the center of this deep of night,
I sit and watch the crumbling stalks and wilted sprouts

as they submerge to the wavering kelp
and shout upon the smacking rains

begging for breath.

In the earliest snip of morning
and the blast of peach colored horizon,

soaked and wet, I leave this mud caked breast of the earth.

Mint

This fragrance in the brush of forest
stretchies across the mountain. I follow this aroma, spice
and take myself to the patch, growth of mint.

So tender, the soil suckles in softness.
Rattling the flavors free as risen from the earth
I suspend myself to each quiver of laughing root.

Gnarled into the thick breeze and loafing gentle leaves,
I wrestle my hands through this passing wind,
eager upon my staining bust and nose.

I follow this trail, path stretching to trembling gasps of wind
becoming the height of a steep mountain,
growing in the earliest of warmth and
blooming to the greens and jades.

Softly, I place a snip of leaf upon the
edge of my watery tongue.

Mothers and Milk

Touching her and hearing her body tremble,
flesh riddling upon flesh,
I croon, devour to her milk filled breasts.

The flinch of her face, teeth gnashing teeth,
I roam each supple crescent curve.

With the height of this Summer's loft
blanching beneath the lemony sun,

I strobe across every pound of her dancing, flinching flesh.
her blood burns hot.

By nightfall, I walk the open fields.
In a swoon, I can hear you moan into the winds,
groom the wheats of every stalk.

With the pulse of the night's quivering skyline,
I still taste the fragrance of your breath.

Beneath

Bold and spirited, I shook to the quivering bones
which rattled beneath my crimping flesh.

Moans from the pit, depth of my threaded chest,
I felt waves of fluid bubble within me.

The glass mirror blinked and I saw the web
of the late Autumn falling mist.

I arrive at this empty field in the deepest of hours.

Walking the carcass of every creek, moan, and groan
of every gnarled wood,

I roam lost into the fibers of these robes which I
discard along the path.

Quivering Summer at the Shores Edge

She dove into the quivering lake,
slippery, her body held each cool drizzle,
I stood by shores edge,

I watched her breasts moisten and her wet brown hair
dredged across her shoulders and back.

I looked past and witnessed the pine woods
roaming to the sky which loafed and tossed
the clouds, thin gauze, upon the dancing gems
of the trembling water and gnarled
chipped cones pelted the earth.

I looked back and she had vanished into the feverish fog.

Sycamore at Summer

The wind tossed the dust of this clay earth.
I hear the echo of my father and his father
As they settled upon a snip of grass and tender green bud.

As I walk through this serene, full meadow,
I feel their loss with every step of my naked feet.

Plush wavering winds threshed through the limbs
Of the wavering sycamore.

Beneath the trunk and sulking branches,
I heard each mumbling voice.

GALAXIES IN THE RAINDROPS

Into the girth of this fattened meadow,
I lay flat and soak beneath the proud pulse of the sun.

Softly, I feel the brooming dust tread from my
Forever slumbering host.

From here, I drift to you in the quiet passion.
I lift as ashes to the sky upon a warm Spring dance.

I bloom to the fragrance of lusty timber.

Sleeping

Steam rose from the pale grass.
From tip to root, the water beads slithered
in faintly spoken words.

From my resting patch, I stood.
I walked the oval stretch of the field
which cleverly held no end.

Into the wetness of the soft grass and root,
these fragrances lulled to the milk of your thighs.

I lightly stepped upon the rivulets of
dancing pools of water, mud.
The naked step of my puckered foot,
I left my stamp, tamp, and press into the lusty meadow.

GALAXIES IN THE RAINDROPS

Beyond,
I drove my way to the bareness of the woodlands.
I delved deeply into vapors
as I faded into the murk and trembling voices
which clamored along the scatter of each stretching pine.

From Ocean to Land

I trembled beneath you, this slithering,
silk water of the ocean.
The endless rows of kelp sauntered across my toe and heel.

Every white cap stroking the waves,
I thought of the nudity of your torso and breasts.

I found my way to where the ripples moan
as a giant, the fury of Poseidon.

As I listened to your groaning, raspy voice;
I heard the labor of your crooning child

Whimpering rasp, thousands upon thousands of years.

In the end, I slumbered with the sirens.
I soaked upon them.

GALAXIES IN THE RAINDROPS

Enveloping their song, I danced to the lyre and spoke
of serendipity and the majus whom forever roams this beach.

I looked to the cliffs and forever sought my way.

By the end, where the waters fade into the
stretches of land, forest, and field,
I quivered to the scent of your foam,
spilling from your breasts.

Photograph

I looked into this photo
and felt my feet deepen into the rich soil.

The sky swelled black and navies as the coarse
wind scattered across the edges of my face.

Mosses and weeds threaded along the cool, damp
flesh which suckled every breeze.

Northern mountains hosted the fresh rain
as I suckled the grip of muds and moist patches.

The hour stood still and tucked every second
into the feverish grip.

I felt the boots press.
In a fraction of a moment, I drifted
across the chambers of the earth.

Night Wishes

Her coat swept across the wooden floor
as I nestled in each fiber of wool.

Faintly, I watched as the vapors filled the room.
I crawled to her and all her nakedness which bent across me

and shook my frame in great trembles of softness;
I danced the sweat from my sleek temples

quietly I fell into the fevers she tossed
tenderly, the promise of daylight crept back into the silent

showers of night.

As the gentle press of her curves and quakes
of her fiery abdomen dripped sauce along each stretch

of my eager flesh, I kissed her upon the quiver of her
well painted lips.

Lost Forever

Silent, lost, I fell so deeply into the mists,
clouded haze of the forest.

The wet touch of the leaves riddled upon me in a soft,
gentle graze as every pouch of bursting pollen

Rolled me into the depth where sweetness
stroked me in malts and flowers quivered beside me.

Deeper yet, the branches full with leaves
grew so thick, I lost the beloved sun

which once would dance along my shoulders and bust,
now I stepped on each gnarled root and branch.

Yet, the mint leaves and sprout of onion gave flavors
as I fell to the soils of the earth and became seduced

with each permeating voice and each tender swish of twig
and dark lash of these heavy gowns.

Paused by the Stream

I paused and looked to the swelling stream.
Hazes of wild blue trellised through the curved, carved water.
The jettison logs mumbled in retort
as every floating stem and stick
quivered their way across the sweet water and bounty.

I stood, found my boot back on it's tread
and ducked into this woodland.

In the brevity and snip of a moment,
I returned to the pampering river and lay
groomed beneath the supple winds as they
courted along this majestic realm.

Since Last Full Moon

Since last month, the moon crumbled to slivers,
then, bloomed and swelled to the fullness
of the moans of each woman whom glazed in it's powders.

I felt the chew of her
as she draped her icy linens upon me.

We fell to a damp press as the murmur of our touch
drizzled a sauce upon us, madenning in this lusty garments.

Onto the ledge of the lumbering stretch of the patio,
I shook to the chill on this fine Spring night
which relished in blossoms and grew rabid by touch.

Warmth spread upon us as the oak and all its leaves gathered
the first splash of daylight and so quickly we weaved
into the shadowed curtains and dust covered bed.

Summer Madness

In the fever of this gushing night, moisture
sobbing on my chest,
I swim through the dampness which brews
through you and fastens me to the
pressures of riddling Summer.

As I watch the tide of you
fumbling into this current, the sweat stained bed,
I share the topics of ancient nightfall
and the moaning verbs which saute between us.

Screams and mumbles of
beyond the buckle and belt,
I swiftly retort to the tang which slithers along my tongue.

Beneath the cascades of your hair I
unstitch to your hem and fibers,

Donny Barilla

roaming through you in the pastures which soothe the winds
outside the tangles of your window.

The most silent touch begins and we gather
each press of flickering moon glances
which tremble and howl.

Endless

Into the woodland, into the deep where moss
crowns the forest floor and leaves bloomed so full,
I ease the sweat stains of my eyes,
I have grown full to the top covered tapestry,
which drips a tender splashing upon me,
soothing in swabbing growth.

The sweetest treat of the onion sprout,
the slither of juice born of the mint leaves
and shrouding gathering of berries,
tenderly, I satiate and by morning, by nightfall.

Donny Barilla

The grip of this gloating, full forest,
I roam my way to the endless edge,
I drink forever from the heavy stream.

I position myself to the drip of each raindrop.
I crumble to the chill of night.

by the end of the dancing rain,
the mulch scents to a rise from the forest floor.

Summer Dust

In the depth of my dream,
I soothed to the touch of her, both fragrance and powder.

She slithered and danced across the patterns and threads
of the linens and wools, downs which glazed
their way across my body, full with sweats.

With window open,
the sweet dusts and scents rose from the garden below
and nursed upon our bodies;
as the winds curved across us,
I breathed into the deep of the fullness of this Summer drift.

Watery beads broke free and glistened along the breadth
of blooming, quiet union.

By morning, I rest, lathered in the wools and fabrics
of my trembling body.

She faded upon the Summer dust.

Slight Return

I felt the bloom, floods of sweet winds which dampened
and swabbed to the pasture of my torso and abdomen.

The creek gloated and filled the clay earth as I sank my feet
and offered a slight return.

The breeze grazed across me as a woman
would graze across me.

I felt the warmth of the blazing sun as it danced
and draped along my slick temples and forehead.

Cupped, the leaves pouched this gathering of dewdrops.

My fullness resumed every pinch of
dust from the tender earth
as I swam through the wind.

Phase to Phase

The stroking bend of Autumn light
threaded across the wheat fields trembling
in harvest tans, browns.

From fields to meadow, I tasted the tangling breads;
steam rose from this trembling place.

With the tamp of my feet, I sulked
and waded through the fields.
By days end, the rain plumped every spot of mud.

I walked through the silk splash of crooning evening
as each mumbling oak spoke to me in it's soft rhythms.

The leaves spoke of the tender sky which
began the powders, snows
blooming upon the narrow path which led me home.

Donny Barilla

The bending branches spoke of each
Winter verb as the dampness
shed so little light.

By the sampling sky, I hushed to the
fragrance which only paused
to rich flavors tossed upon with the early Spring sky.

Sweat showered each pollen and quivering
bud, eager in the color jaded
and stroked emerald upon this flushing, dancing sun.

I sliced the carving moon upon nightfall
and softly I fell to sleep with endless beds of grass and sprout.

Swabbing along a most humid flash where
pollens fed the dancing stalk
and wavering husk.

Edge

The quivering lilacs shook through each groan
of each pampering breeze, blooming in the most
delicate colors and murmuring stems.

Pollens took flight and answwered in skyward moans
which hooked a soft delicate seed,
soft upon the earth.

I deepened my fingers into the moist
treads and bushel of leaves
as the proud richness of muds and
minerals proclaimed their health
with the snap of the winds upon the tender sky.

When the rain sobbed through each
blush of quivering clouds,

Donny Barilla

I fell to the base of the maple and slowly breathed
their saps and syrups- by nightfall I knelt upon the earth.

I darkened my way to the groin where
each drifting burst of pod
shook loose to the woods and all their masquerade.

Into the tension of this thick hunger and shadow,
the silence broomed the shudders which stemmed
their way through the forest's edge.

Satin Glades

The words fell from the swoon of the fallen garment
which only moan their way through the shadow
of this down and silk linens.

Fingers weave as the hush of tender nightfall
brooms dust through the trembling breath of echo and retort.

From the silent shake of the flesh of each abdomen,
their lurks a dance which only plumes in the black
of tender trembling night.

Leaving in the quiver of morning,
shimmer of the earliest dust, I walk the wooden floor
and think of each touch you belong to
in this shout and parade of sun which dances
across the satin glades.

Pillow

The roof and walls rattled with the most punishing winds.
Near the window, the maple smacked branch upon branch.

I heard the depth of the soil mumble with every
flood and trace of flood.

I leaned my head into this generous pillow.
So sweetly I fastened to the feathered grip.

In a swift saunter, I fell upon the wind.

Ocean's Gallery

The evening sky slithered through the thinning clouds,
alive the colors of apricots and tender these heaviest
of wine grapes.

The silk ocean's sand demanded the foams which whimper
along every pebble and shell.

I absorb the pulse of the warm air, the humid breath
striding across the waters which groom
my soft, freshened mouth.

By morning, I walked into the full naked dunes;
I sank my hands with smooth trust as the peach hues
grew sullen upon the grip of my quivering palm.

Donny Barilla

The teardrops fell upon the haze of this delicately fogged
waters edge.

Turning south, I gingerly walked, then
paused, then walked again.

The jaw of the sky, dripped humid as the
mist blanched my arms and bust.

Realm

Auburn hair which flooded across her pale, powder white shoulders mimicked to the clever boast of the horizon.

Breasts trimmed the alabaster of her soft, fragrant flesh opened me to a softer realm where branches stand still and wind lulls to a most gentle breath.

In her younger youth, there brewed lava beneath her skin and tempests which threshed upon her lusty hair.

Pampering lips dashed about me as the
coined treasure of her tongue
trembled across the field soaked and naked beyond her home.

Donny Barilla

In the turn of my gaze, I swept each finger of each hand
and trembled beneath the spread where
she gifted her moisture.

By the gush of the thickest part of
night, I rose upon the husks
from the neighboring maize and flooded with each
watery parcel of my hungry mouth.

Lusty Flood

I stand among this shroud of dust,
fading to the trembling wind.
Clay mounds burn from toes to the edge of my heel.

Later, the moist air loosened tears upon the earth
which moaned at each movement and scattering leaf.

The sky bled fast the color lemon and pink.
beneath, I stood in the drip of the harvest sky;
I leaned back and gathered rain into the goblet of my mouth

which yearned for the summit of her
proud, drifting gown, blouse.

Donny Barilla

Her voice leveled as the drift of the fading breeze.
Her breath was a damp gathering of
moss and stroking shrubs
which tenderized at the crimp of my dipped feet and ankles.

I turned to the onslaught of the moaning winds.
Tender, I loosened my crouching stance
and entered this lusty flood.

Apple Groves

I shook loose the webbed rain of this fallen cloud,
perched, I fastened to the dampest of boulders
smoothed beneath my wavering feet.

Tender, I bloomed the sweetest drips from her edge,
corner of her mouth.

By each parched patch of grass, the moisture
which bled through the swollen sky,
fattened my silent appetite
into the grains of her spice laden and fragrant hair.

Now quite early the next slumbering
morning, dancing daylight,
I walked across these fleshy hills which bloomed
heavy in apple groves surrounded by pines which
softly shed their cones into a chipped mound.

Waiting for Morning

I turned to the breath of you and poured
across each bend and curve
as the shore flooded in sweet, humid
presses, alive here at the crimp
of the deepest pinch where nighttime
sulks through every damp bloom.

Tamped into your nakedness, I spoke to you upon the chill
called, "night."

Tumbling in every pause and touch of the hand,
I kissed your trembling belly and discovered
each edge of the universe.

With window open, I smelled the fertile soil
which saurated the blossomed lilac-
flooding aromas in the heavy garden.

Into the champion blast of heat, the mask of morning,
I swept the blanket, pulsed the down pillow.
Roaming through this pleasure, I gripped the dancing light.

Ocean Timepiece

From clifftop to ocean spread,
fangs scoured into the water and all it's waistline;
alive these puckering salts, warm and thick,
spray rose upon the cheeks and bones of my face.

The wind broomed me across every pinch.
Swift, I returned to the rocks and waves from where I belong.

I corned to the tumbling white caps as they flung
quick in the grip of high tide.

I responded to the buoys, blundering as this silent guest.

At the towering width of the lighthouse,
I swelled to every ocean shore, plucked in this timepiece
of weathered dance.

Threshold

I never cross this space between us,
forever blooming upon this threshold
which burrows into the crest, from moon to pulsing sun.

As the wilted leaf leaned to the quiet, silent earth,
I delve through thin masked air and reach for your breasts,
never touching.

Your powders fill my face, yet the sculpted chisel
of your shoulders remain remote,
bloomed upon the foggy drip of cloud and tense air.

I come to you in the press of every grass blade
filled in the fumbling open field.

I taste you as the night skyline vanishes and
I awaken to the tremble of daylight.

Thread to Thread

The sky tore from thread to thread.
as the sweet rain tapped the once quiet earth,
I listened to you as you spoke of the rivers you flood
and the ponds, lakes you swelled.

With the pasted brown hair sulked upon
my head, neck, and shoulders,
I offered you deliberation and retort.

With mumbling shouts of the drenched soils
of the buttered earth,
you spoke of touch and you breathed across the dripping
chill of my ears.

I plunged into you as the damp, darkness of night
swabbed across me in fog, drifting gauze and the tremble
of a soft cottony wind.

About the Author

Donny Barilla, a poet covering the realms: human intimacy, nature, mythology, theology, and man's relationship with death and the departed, has been writing for over three decades. He writes daily and strives to renew himself as an artist from page to page and body of work to body of work. Very seldom does he take a break from writing as he views it as a full-time job. He lives a reclusive lifestyle and finds himself clinging close to nature and all her elements. His home state of Pennsylvania strikes chords of poetic depth about him as he finds loveliness from cornfield to meadow. Whether it's feelings of love, intimacy, or a special closeness, he maintains the feeling that death does not take these with him/her to the grave. Emotions and feeling outlast the flesh of the human body. Human intimacy draws near an enigmatic spiritual passion which conquers all on the prismatic scale of experience. When speaking of mythology Donny says, "myths were created to make sense of feelings which are complicated by very nature. They are perhaps more easily understood through persons greater than oneself. As for theology, a disciplined aspect, incorporates quite finely with passions and secured poetic comforts.

https://twitter.com/BarillaDonny

www.ingramcontent.com/pod-product-compliance
Lightning Source LLC
Chambersburg PA
CBHW031432160426
43195CB00010BB/706